AMANDA VAN ANNAN

Win The RUNWAY

A Practical Guide On How To Make It To The
Top Of The Modelling Industry And Stay There

So, You Want to Be a Model?

This book is dedicated to the women in my life

To my mother who could not be there

To my step mum for keeping me alive

To my aunt who made me realize I could dream

To my sisters for always being there

To my darling grandma for telling me with faith all things are possible.

To my cousin whose light shone so bright

To my friends who became family.

To the models, the bookers, the agents, managers, make-up artists, photographers, stylists , clients and of course the party promoters.

All the amazing people I met along the way and also the ones that were so insecure they forced me to become a stronger person and stand for change.

Some we are still in touch and others our paths never crossed again. Modeling is one of the most exciting life journeys one will ever have.

It's a journey of self-discovery through travel,growing pains and sometimes being thrown in unusual situations. Like life, modeling can be challenging yet very satisfying.   This book is for all of you, the tried, the tested and the true.

Stay focused, enjoy the journey, it is one of human connection, fragility and sometimes human misbehavior.

Table of Contents

Preface

While sitting in my NYC apartment thinking about writing a book to help future models succeed in their modeling careers, a thought came to mind. The modeling industry has changed so much since I started modeling in the early 2000s. In the '90s, supermodels were featured on the pages and covers of magazines, Cindy Crawford, Christy Turlington, Helena Christensen, Naomi Campbell, Tatjana Patitz, and Elaine Erwin, to just name a few. This was probably the golden era of modeling.

I started modeling at the young age of 17, and by the time I was 18, I was in Paris, far away from home, and on the international runways of the world. I was young, I was naïve, but I was also lucky. I worked for a top model agency called Metropolitan Models. I was lucky enough to have my career take off, and was always busy flying to places as far afield as South Africa, Athens, and even Japan.

The purpose of this book is not only to give you a road map to modeling but to also provide you with a blueprint that you can always refer to. Things are constantly changing in the modeling and fashion industry. One minute it is all about being super-chic, and the next, it's all about streetwear.

The good news today is that unlike in my time when you practically had to be a unicorn and represented by an agency to be a model, the doors have now opened to anyone and everyone. Modeling is about having an identity, paving it forward, revealing your true authenticity, and being present. By doing this, you show up as the best possible version of yourself.

The best possible version of yourself is your best self, the one that does not hide from anyone and is your true, authentic self. Models today have to be more than a pretty face; you have to ooze personality and have a presence. With many social media apps, you can create a whole brand, starting from nothing and building it into something.

I decided to write this book to be your bible and help guarantee your success in this cut-throat industry. Modeling is not an easy game. To be honest, luck has a lot to do with it. You have to have a lot of stars aligned if you want to make it in this industry. In this book, I attempt to make your journey easier by giving you practical advice to help you navigate your path through the modeling world. I also advise you on the best actions to take to give your career an exponential kick start and keep you a step ahead of the rest.

Win the runway is a book you should always keep close at hand. I talk about safety, personal branding, finding an agent, perseverance, and a whole lot more. The book ends with a section on hacks that can help you find an agent fast or help you book a job. Some of these hacks are one of a kind, and you have to be brave to execute them, but who said there was anything wrong with being brave and positive? These hacks will get you through the door, and at least, get you seen.

I also provide a list of modeling agencies in major cities as well as tips to launch your career even if you do not have an agent. Remember that you are worth it, and you can launch a whole modeling career even if you do not have an agency. The key is to start thinking of yourself as a brand and pinpointing your attributes. You do not have to be famous to be a brand; you can create your brand and find a tribe of people that will follow you and identify themselves with your brand.

When reading this book, you may feel as if some of the information I provide is repetitive; but, there is a method behind this—I want to instill the basic building blocks about the modeling industry in you so you stand a better chance of success. There are bonus chapters with several hacks that can help put you ahead of your competition, so follow them carefully and diligently. Modeling, like any other job you plan to make money from, requires focus and sheer determination.

I am so happy to be your guide and coach on your journey to success. Remember: the game has changed, so don't let anyone call the shots for you. If they say that you can't keep focused and stay focused, remember that can.

When you read this book, please read slowly, make notes, and then read it repeatedly. If you need any advice, you can contact my team at team@wintherunway.com. I will try my best to reply and answer your questions.

I look forward to seeing you on the cover of a magazine, in a TV commercial, in a print advert, or on Instagram. Yes, you can do this, and I hope to be your guide on this journey with you.

With love,

Amanda

C H A P T E R   O N E

What is a model?

Since the beginning of time, humans have always been fascinated with fashion. Fashion started when people began wearing clothes, dating back 100,000-500,000 years. Over the centuries, clothing became a way of conveying social status and individuality. But the days of haute couture are slowly disappearing with the emergence of mass-produced, ready-to-wear clothing.

Modeling, as a profession, was first established in 1853 by Charles Frederick Worth, the "father of haute couture," when he asked his wife, Marie Vernet Worth, to model the clothes he designed. Marie attracted the attention of the ladies of the French court and then the Empress Eugénie herself, by wearing Worth's creations. From then on, Worth became a pioneer in designing dresses that were distributed across the world.

A model can be defined as anyone who puts on clothes, accessories, or undergarments and shows them off to others; yet this description can be somewhat narrow. Since the 1800s, modeling has evolved, and there are so many different types of models. This includes commercial models, runway models, editorial models, hand models, face models, and the list goes on. The business of modeling usually refers to someone that is generally a clothes model, even though they may also do some other type of modeling.

CHAPTER TWO

Who can be a model?

Generally speaking, almost anyone can be a model. That being said, there are different criteria depending on the type of modeling you plan to go into. The most popular of all modeling disciplines, as mentioned above, is fashion modeling, closely followed by commercial modeling. For anyone looking to make a career out of modeling, my advice would be to stick to one of these two modeling disciplines.

Now, back to the question: who can be a model?

The criteria are different for both types of modeling. First, let's talk about fashion modeling. To be a fashion model, you usually have to be a minimum height of five-foot nine-inches for women and five-foot ten-inches for men. Though this is the standard height, there have been models that are shorter who have become very successful as fashion models. Two such examples are British models Kate Moss and Cara Delevingne.

As a fashion model, you are required to be about an American size four to six or a British size eight to ten. That being said, these days, you can also be a plus-size model. Most plus-size models are about an American size ten to twelve or a British size fourteen to sixteen. Appearance also matters in the realm of fashion modeling, but you don't necessarily have to be the prettiest. You could be quirky, unusual, or different-looking. Agents often look for models that look different.

Commercial modeling, on the other hand, caters to all shapes and sizes. Commercial models are usually referred to as the girl or boy next door. This means that you can be any shape or size. Commercial models are used in commercials, Ad campaigns, and catalogs for various brands. As a commercial model, the most important thing you should do is to make sure you have good skin, hair, and nails. Good skin is a prerequisite for all types of modeling, so always make sure you take good care of your skin. Good skin is essential, especially as some shoots require close ups, so maintaining a good skincare regime is a must.

Cara Delevigne

CHAPTER THREE

Types of Modeling

As stated earlier, there are various types of modeling. I will first give you a brief description of each type, and in a later chapter, we will expand on this some more. One thing to take note of is that since the advent of social media, there has been a lot of new developments in the modeling arena, and new categories of models have emerged.

Different types of models:

- Runway Model

    Runway models are fashion models who model clothing on a catwalk. They walk up and down the runway in garments, modeling them on the catwalk for an audience. Runway modeling is probably the most difficult of all the modeling categories as you have to be of a particular body type, usually tall (five-foot-nine and above), and thin.

    Runway modeling can be a lot of fun, especially because top models get to travel worldwide and do fashion shows for big brands like Gucci, Louis Vuitton, Chanel, Prada, and so many more. The four main markets for runway models are New York, London, Paris, and Milan; however, this does not mean that you have to travel to these markets to start your career. We will talk more about runway modeling and what you need to know if you decide to be a runway model in a later chapter.

- Commercial Model

    We have talked a lot about commercial models. Commercial models are the girls and boys next door. You don't have to be tall, thin, or look a certain way to be a commercial model — anyone can be a commercial model because commercial models come in all shapes and sizes.

    Just look at television commercials and you will see different kinds of people of all shapes and sizes. If you want to get into this type of modeling, you need good, professional photos. Build a small portfolio of professional photos showcasing you smiling and let your character and personality shine. Remember, your modeling portfolio may be one of your most important assets. In the past, portfolios were made up of what was referred to as a "Model Book." These were photo albums of your best photos, curated so that clients could see them when you go on appointments.

- IG Models (influencers)

    The IG model phenomenon is the latest type of modeling. It has disrupted the modeling industry over the last five years. IG is an acronym for Instagram and an IG model means an Instagram model. Instagram is a social media application owned by Facebook on which everyone can go to curate photos of their lives.

When Instagram launched, many people started posting photos, and as they posted, they got followers. Some of them got more followers than others. As people got more followers on Instagram, some advertisers and companies started approaching them to advertise their goods, creating a new market of Instagram models and influencers.

The good news about becoming an Instagram model is that you do not need an agent to start; however, the process is rather difficult now that the market has become saturated. So, you will need to create a well-curated Instagram account and engage with your followers daily, as well as post at least three times a week to build your following.

Some models have used Instagram to help them find agents. They start out posting on Instagram and clients and modeling agencies approach them for work. Another good thing about Instagram modeling is that you can create your own identity and just be yourself. Sometimes, people are drawn to your individual character. Instagram can also be used as a digital portfolio, and you can send agents and clients there to look at your work and find out more about you.

- Plus-Size Modeling

When fashion modeling initially started, most models had to be a standard size, mainly because most designers designed their clothing to certain specifications. Models had to be a certain height and a certain clothing size to fit into the designer's clothes. Though women come in all shapes and sizes, the industry did not consider this, and you could say that it was rather biased and one-sided.

But since then, a lot of things have changed. Models (especially, commercial models) come in all shapes and sizes. Plus-size modeling is modeling for larger, fuller-figured men and women. The plus-size modeling industry is a growing market, and most traditional modeling agencies now have plus-size models. There are famous plus-size models you may know like Sophie Dahl and Ashley Green.

To become a plus-size model, you have to take the same steps as you would when trying to get into fashion or commercial modeling. The first thing to do is find an agent or manager (if you want one). As with fashion modeling, you can start taking shots and posting on Instagram. Getting professional photos will help you get an agent quicker, as this will show them how you look in print.

As well as photos, you can create a slate video. Slates help potential agents and managers see what you look like on video, and the photos let them know what you look like on camera or in a flat image. To make a "slate" video, you record a video of you stating your name, height, measurements, and a bit about yourself. You then turn so they can see your left and right profiles. When you have created the slate video, you are ready to send your photos out to agents and managers.

- Editorial Models

I am sure that the first place you probably noticed a fashion model was in a magazine, on a billboard, or on the runway. Editorial models are those frequently featured in magazines including Vogue, Elle, Marie Claire, and Cosmopolitan. Most fashion models do both runway and editorial modeling. But some models tend to either be more editorial or do more runway. Both types of modeling cross over, usually because the same designers featured in magazine editorials also do runway shows. Editorials are magazine photo stories that use mostly designer clothes. Editorial magazines are commonly known as fashion magazines for this very reason.

So, we could conclude by saying that editorial modeling is the same as fashion modeling, as we mentioned earlier in this book. To become an editorial model, you have to join a mainstream fashion modeling agency as most magazines almost exclusively book models through modeling agencies. At the end of this book, I will give you a list of fashion modeling agencies in an accompanying workbook, as well as links to a lot of resources that may be helpful in the modeling world.

• Male Models

When most people think of models, they usually think of female models, but in the last 25 years, the male fashion modeling industry has grown exponentially. In the past, people did not think that male modeling was a real job, but decades have passed, and that mindset has changed. There are many successful male models in all fields of modeling today, so when I talk about modeling, I refer to both male and female models, and not just female models per se. The modeling industry is for everyone, regardless of race, gender, or physical characteristics. Most agencies represent both male and female models.

- Child Modeling

Fashion models usually start their careers around the age of 15 but "commercial models" can start at any age. Most commercials feature people from different age groups so commercial models that appear in catalogs or on TV can start their career at any age.

There are certain rules and restrictions that pertain to child models. This differs in various countries and also in different states. But one universal rule is that a parent or guardian must supervise child models. In a future chapter, I will explain more about child modeling and give you some basic guidelines as they pertain to this aspect of modeling.

Child modeling can be fun for both parent and child. Still, it is not necessarily as easy as you think as it involves taking the child to auditions, castings, callbacks, fittings, and accompanying them on set and shoots. That said, modeling as a child can be a great start to a successful modeling career.

CHAPTER FOUR

Modeling agents – Do I really need one?

Modeling agents represent models to help them find work and guide their careers by liaising with future clients and negotiating contracts. But one question that a lot of people ask is, "Do I actually need representation?" Well, my answer to this is yes and no. Many clients book directly through modeling agents, which gives models access to a broader pool of work opportunities. There are also a lot of complexities in terms of contractual and payment obligations. You will need someone who can draft contracts for clients and is well-versed when it comes to making sure that you are paid fairly. Some model platforms, actually have contracts that models can print out and give clients and have special services to help models draft contracts.

Instead of a modeling agent, you can be represented by a parent, relative, or family friend who is familiar with drawing up legal contracts and can actively look for and schedule work for you. When it comes to looking for work as a model, a lot has changed since the advent of social media. A lot of clients now scan through social media apps like Instagram and TikTok when looking for models. You can always start out on social media, but please be safe and careful. It may be a good idea to have a parent or family member help you curate your photos on social media and monitor your social media accounts, so you have a second pair of eyes to look over your photos and following.

As well as advertising your modeling on social media, you can also create profiles on different modeling platforms, or create your own website. However, one advantage to having a modeling agent is that all clients are properly vetted so you don't have this kind of security when sourcing your own clients. You will need to do thorough research before approaching a potential client.

If you're actively looking for a modeling agent, first it would be a good idea to start thinking about where you might fit in. Start looking through magazines, watching television, and scanning social media to get an idea. This will give you a clue about which agents to search for depending on the type of criteria they're looking for in terms of appearance, size, and trend. But when looking at an agent's website please do not use the modeling images you see as your only guide as it is not always a cookie-cutter approach as far as modeling goes. Just because you don't look like the images you see does not mean that a model agent is not looking for someone just like you.

Another good tip is to start taking care of your skin earlier on. Remember that agents want models with good skin, so the earlier you start taking care of your skin, the better. We will discuss finding an agent and what agents are looking for in-depth in a later chapter.

CHAPTER   FIVE

How to find a modeling agent

Finding a modeling agent can be challenging, but persistence is key. You have to remember that modeling agencies can only represent a limited number of models at any given time which means you may have to meet several agents before signing with one. This also means that agents are particular about who they sign. But even if you are signed to a modeling agent, this does not necessarily mean that you will start working straight away. A modeling agent is not an employer but an agent representing you, and you have to do your part to get work. Your "part" includes making sure you provide all of the tools the agent needs, including shooting with recommended photographers, making sure your skin looks good, exercising regularly, and also looking for jobs and opportunities on your own.

There are many ways to look for job opportunities and get yourself out there. social media is a great starting point. Through social media sites like Instagram, you can build your very own portfolio of photos and really display your personality. Many clients scout and approach models directly on social media so I would definitely work on your social media presence. Uploading your portfolio on different modeling platforms is another great way to increase your exposure and seek modeling work. There are many modeling platforms including Keamod.com, swipecast.com, starnow.com, modelsdirect.com, modelmanagement. com, and allcasting.com that represent photographers, makeup artists, and stylists.

If you are thinking about representing yourself and using social media, do remember to be safe online and be careful about who you give your personal information to. One disadvantage of sourcing your own work through social media is that it is difficult for models to correctly vet and perform security checks on clients.

As mentioned earlier, you either fall into the fashion model or the commercial model category, and both types of modeling have different approaches:

Commercial agents

Commercial modeling is a broader and more general type of modeling compared to other types. They represent all types of models, so commercial models tend to be more like the average girl or boy next door. Anyone can be a commercial model, and commercial modeling agencies are always looking for different people to represent. But some agents may prefer having only one or two models with the same look. For example, you may be rejected by commercial agents because they already represent someone that looks similar to you. This is not bad news; all you have to do is go and see another commercial agent.

Commercial modeling is often compared with high-fashion or editorial modeling, but these are not the same. Unlike fashion modeling, for commercial modeling, I would advise you to build a small portfolio of professional photos of you wearing day-to-day clothes and showing off your personality which will really grab the attention of an agent. Commercial agencies like to see professional images because they usually do not develop you as a talent, but rather, they send you on commercial or print auditions to get work, so they like to see what you will look like in a commercial or print advert. Some commercial models even take acting classes as this helps with television commercials, but acting classes are not necessary, as most commercial modeling gigs are print jobs. Compile a list of commercial agents and call them to see what their requirements are. Some agencies have open-calls once a week or month where potential new models can come in to see them and the agency can decide if they can sign them. You can usually find out about open-calls on the agency's website. If you are under 18, please make sure you attend with a parent or guardian and never sign any paperwork with an agent without adult supervision. Some agencies, on the other hand, may ask potential future models to send in photos of themselves before deciding if they want to represent them or not.

Remember that commercial agents prefer more natural-looking models. When meeting a commercial agent, you have to go in as you are, naturally. There is no need to put on excess makeup or be overly done-up. When you have a meeting with a commercial agent, go in casually; they are interested in your personality more than anything else, so going in and being personable will be a bonus. One thing I must emphasize through all of this is that you should not take anything personally in the modeling arena. Some agents may be rude, or they may not be the most sociable, but it has nothing to do with you. They are busy people.

Remember that many models are trying to get agents every day, so if they do not sign you the first time, try again in the future. If you are determined, you will eventually find an agent, and they will notice your passion and enthusiasm.

Fashion runway and editorial agents

High-fashion models are usually classified as editorial and/or runway models and are hired to model the fashion designs of high-end fashion designers. This is one of the highest-paid modeling categories.

High-fashion models are rare because most aspiring male and female models do not meet the high-standard required. To be a high-fashion model you generally must be five-foot-nine and above and have a different look about you, but this look does not necessarily mean that high-fashion models are the most beautiful or handsome. Even though runway models may have a different look or facial appearance, they all have to be a similar body shape. These models tend to have a lean body type and very thin arms and legs, kind of like mannequins in a shop.

Let me mention here that you do not have to be super-skinny or anything like that, but you have to be between an American size two and four or a UK size six to eight, at least five-foot-nine and have good skin and nice teeth.

Like commercial modeling, fashion models are usually represented by agents, though you can build your own portfolio on social media or upload it on a modeling platform.

Fashion modeling agents are usually not looking for you to already be established so when approaching a fashion modeling agency, you don't necessarily have to have your whole portfolio together. Your agent will schedule for you to do test shoots with photographers to build your portfolio. My advice would be to save your money on expensive professional photos and just send agents regular photos or polaroids with your full face and hair behind your ears and some images with your hair down. A white t-shirt (preferably white) and a pair of shorts are ideal so agents can see your legs. Stand in front of a bare, white wall and make sure you have good lighting. Do a few face shots, some three-quarter length shots, some full-body shots, and make sure you take some profile views too. Once you have your simple, well-lit photos, send them to a few agencies to see how they respond. You can find a list of modeling agencies in your area by doing a simple Google search.

Modeling agents may also require you to do a video of yourself and send it to them. The video is usually a slate and a profile view in which you look at the camera, say your name and height, turn left, turn right, and give them a full 360-degree turn. You also usually say a bit about yourself. The video should be no more than two to three minutes. It gives the agent an idea of what you look like on film and your personality.

There are parts of fashion modeling that could cross over with commercial modeling, and some fashion models do end up having successful commercial modeling careers.

As we have discussed, there are many advantages of being represented by a modeling agent. Most clients trust agents and directly book models through them. As well as sourcing work, modeling agents also manage your schedule, deal with contracts, and ensure all clients are vetted. But if you do not succeed in finding an agent, this should not stop you from starting to build your portfolio online and trying to look for work yourself as a freelance model.

CHAPTER SIX

How to find your own modeling work

There are many ways to increase your exposure and source your own modeling work. All you need is a website, a social media page, good photographs, and contact details.

- Your Website

    When thinking about creating a website, keep it simple. Remember that your potential clients are going to your website to see your work, see what you can do, how you photograph, and if you are suitable to cast for a job.

    A good and easy way to create a personal website is using wix.com. Wix has hundreds of different website templates and step by step instructions you can use to build your website. Choose a template that is minimal and clean. Your website should have different sections on different pages including an "about" section, sections on commercial and editorial modeling, a portfolio, a contact information page, and a review section.

In the "about" section you should tell people a bit about yourself, who you are, and where you are from. The website should have all your measurements namely, your height, dress size, shoe size, trouser inseam, eye color, hair color, waist, bust, and hip measurements. For male models, you do not need to include a bust or hip measurement, but you will need your shirt size, shoulder width, and chest dimensions. Make sure you also include your contact information but please do not put a physical address on the website unless it is the office address of the agency representing you (if you have an agent). Generally, addresses are not advised on websites for security reasons.

An essential part of your website is, of course, good photographs. Your photos have to be professionally taken. You can find a list of photographers by using Google or social media. When shooting with a photographer you have never met before, please make sure an adult is with you at the shoot or location. Photographers that shoot models are usually used to shooting new faces. They will usually organize a makeup artist for you, and in some cases, a stylist as well. You will not need a stylist for commercial modeling, as you just have to shoot in your normal day-to-day wear. This may also apply to fashion modeling, as some of your photos could also be in everyday clothes but more stylized.

Remember your website is a representation of yourself, so put your best foot forward.

- Modeling Platforms

You can jumpstart your modeling career by joining a modeling platform. Modeling platforms exist all over the world and are a great way to see what is going on in the modeling industry and give you an idea of what competition is out there. Clients go on to modeling platforms, search for models, contact them, and book them for work. Modeling platforms allow you to upload your portfolio, your measurements, and a video of you, and then you are then in a marketplace where potential clients and photographers can find you.

The good news is that you may get photographers approach you and ask to shoot you for free once you have a portfolio. This is called test shooting. A test shoot is where the photographer or team has a particular vision or project in mind that they want to shoot, and they book a model to help them achieve their vision. Test shoots are great as they help you build your modeling portfolio. So if a photographer asks you for a test shoot and you like what he intends to shoot, definitely do the shoot as it will help develop your modeling portfolio.

At this point, I must mention that the modeling game is not easy. It requires dedication, perseverance, and hard work, so stay focused. Modeling is not for everyone. It can be very challenging, and the work may be inconsistent, so it may not be a way to make a steady income. I always personally advise young models to stay in school at the beginning of their modeling career, unless they are scouted by a top agency that will manage their careers and try to push them to the top of the game.

- Social Media

In the past, if a model did not have an agent, they had no way to launch a modeling career on their own, mainly because clients only booked through modeling agencies. But with the advent of social media, models are now finding work themselves. Clients are more open to booking models without agents and model scouts often use social media to find new models. Most clients still prefer going through agents because it is more convenient and the legal paperwork is easier to handle as agents have all the legal verbiage and know what fees to charge for various jobs. That said, social media, particularly Instagram, is still a good way to jumpstart your career in all modeling fields as you can upload photos and videos of yourself modeling onto your social media page. You can create a virtual portfolio on social media and send the URL link to potential clients.

Your main intent is to use social media as your modeling platform. You have to curate your modeling photos, so they stand out. If you have professional photos, use them. If you don't, and you can't afford to shoot professionally, get a friend to shoot you. If you are interested in being a catwalk model, you can put videos of yourself walking on your social media too. Social media is an excellent way to let people know you exist and that you are around.

- Model Scouts

A model scout usually has relationships with agencies and goes out scouting models for one or more agencies. Some model scouts work independently and when they find new talent, they set them up with an agency or a manager. You can meet a model scout anywhere, through social media, at modeling conferences, or they might even approach you on the street. If you're young, they usually ask to speak to your parents and will tell them that they are interested in you joining their agency. Naomi Campbell, for example, was scouted at the age of 15 in Covent Garden, London, on her way home from school. She joined Elite Model Management and became one of the most significant models in history.

Please note that if a model scout approaches you, please do not go anywhere with them. You can ask for their business card and tell them that you will be in touch. A real model scout will have a business card on them.

- Modeling Conferences

Many modeling conferences take place in the USA and all around the world. The biggest one of them all is the Modeling Association of America conference that takes place yearly. This conference has a lot of modeling agents and talent scouts from all over the USA. Attending modeling conferences is a great way for potential models to gain a deeper insight into the whole modeling game and the modeling industry. You get a real feel for what it might be like in the industry. At modeling conferences, you can meet several agencies under one roof, and it can save you the time and effort of trying to find an agent as you will be able to meet agents from all over the world.

Modeling conferences are worth attending at least once as they give you real-time, face-to-face insight into the industry, and you can meet the industry's players.

CHAPTER SEVEN

What do modeling agents look for?

So, what do modeling agencies look for when they think of signing on a model? Modeling agencies have different criteria they use to determine if they want to sign a model or not.

- The Look

    Some modeling agencies prefer a certain look. For example, most editorial and runway models have chiseled or pronounced features whereas commercial agencies prefer more natural, plainer-looking people. Each agency may have a specific look they prefer, depending on if it represents fashion models, commercial models, plus-size models, or character models.

You have to start thinking about which model category you will fit into. Some models are lucky enough to have a generic look that crosses over into fashion modeling and commercial modeling.

When approaching an agency as a new model, they want you to see simple photos, as we discussed earlier, showing your face, your body, and different profiles. You do not need to have heavy, stylized images; they want to see raw, fresh photos.

What is a fresh look?

A fresh look literally means your look without makeup or with very little makeup. They want to see you in the most natural state, not overly made up or excessively stylized. Your photos should be in a simple white T-shirt with a pair of jean shorts, or a nice, simple dress. For men, a white T-shirt, and a pair of jeans.

Remember: keep it simple.

- Polaroids

    When you go in to see an agent, they will usually take a photo of you with their Polaroid camera. They will normally tell you to stand against a wall to take a basic snapshot. This is so they can see your bone structure in a simple photograph and see what you would look like with makeup or in a shoot. Some agencies use digital cameras now, but in the olden days, polaroids were the big thing. Remember that these people are experts, and they know the business inside and out. They have an expert eye. They want to see a raw canvas and build it up.

- Height Requirements

    We have briefly talked about height requirements. For commercial models, height does not matter as much, but editorial and fashion models usually have to be at least five-foot-nine, though some shorter models have become successful in this field, like Kate Moss and Cara Delevingne. If you are a bit shorter but have the right look, you may still get into a fashion modeling agency. It all depends on what they are looking for when you go into the agency. However, if fashion modeling does not work for you, you can try commercial modeling, as this may be a more easily accessible option for you.

- Plus-size Models

    Though most modeling agencies prefer more average-sized models and thinner types, commercial agencies, as mentioned before, represent all shapes and sizes. There are also specific agencies that represent larger girls, called plus-size agencies.

    Some fashion modeling agencies also have plus size divisions that represent models like Ashley Greene—a very successful plus-size model. Being a plus-size model can be just as fun and lucrative as being an average model. Plus-size models are getting used more and more these days in high profile jobs, as they are a real representation of the general populace.

- Age

    In commercial modeling, age does not matter. This is because, as mentioned earlier, commercial agencies represent a mass cross-section of people. Commercials have all types of people of different ages, so commercial agencies need to represent all people.

However, when it comes to fashion modeling, it can be a bit more discriminatory. For those who are starting a fashion modeling career, agencies look for new faces between the ages of 15 to 19 for women and 16 to 23 for men; but don't let this stop you if you are older or younger. Sometimes, older people approach agencies and get signed by them.

In general, fashion modeling has a brief shelf life that usually ends when women are in their early thirties, while men can model into their fifties. This is changing, but not as fast as it should.

• Availability

Once you sign with a model agency, they will want to know your availability as they need to know if you are available for jobs, castings, and to meet with new clients on go-sees. Some younger models that are still in school usually model during vacation time as they cannot take time off school.

For commercial models, the availability issue is less of a problem as commercial auditions don't come up as much. But for fashion models, castings and go-sees happen daily. Sometimes, clients request to see models if they intend to use them for a particular shoot or job, so your availability is important to model agents as they need to know when they can send you out on castings and when you are unavailable.

You can check-out of the agency when you are unavailable, and when you are available, you can check back in. When you check-out, your agent will mark you as unavailable during that time.

- Behavior

  One last thing I want to talk about is behavior and attitude. As a model, you are going to meet a lot of people so please always try to be cordial and professional. If there is an incident of any sort or there is an issue with a fellow model, call your agency straight away and inform an adult guardian if you are a minor. Bullying is not tolerated and will not be allowed.

  Your attitude will also help you get work. People generally like to help people with whom they feel comfortable. If you are the shy type and don't talk much, try to build your confidence. You don't have to be bubbly, but you have to be friendly. Don't be rude. Turn up on time for your appointments, and always let the agency know if you are running late or can't make an appointment. Modeling is a people's profession, as you work with so many teams of people on set, so try to learn how to be cordial at least.

- Portfolios

  A modeling portfolio may be one of your most important assets as a model. A portfolio will usually be leather or plastic-bound approximately 20 inches by 14 inches in size with plastic sleeves inside where you can slide your modeling photos into. These plastic sleeves are see-through and look just like a photo album. Portfolios were originally called "Model Books" and were about 30 inches by 20 inches, and models used to lug them everywhere. As of recent, most models have their portfolios on iPads, as everything has now gone digital. It does make it much easier to carry around.

  In your portfolio, you should include your best photos. These photos represent the market you are targeting. For example, a swimsuit model will have photos showing their body in swimsuits, an editorial model, on the other hand, will have mostly fashion photos, and a commercial model will have very natural, girl or boy next door type photos. As well as photos, your portfolio may also include tear-sheets which are pages from editorial, and photos and clippings from previous commercial shoots you have done. Tear-sheets are important as they show clients that you are a working model.

At the very front of your portfolio should be a sleeve to hold your Z-card. A modeling Z-card can be compared to a business card. When you meet a future client or go on castings, they look through your book, and you leave them a Z-card. This Z-card is what they use to remember you. Z-cards are useful in that sense, as they represent your body of work and they are left with the client. Z-cards are about five inches by seven inches in size. The front of the car has your name and a close-up photo of you and the back has your measurements and two to four other photos of you on it.

Agencies use different formats for their Z-cards. Although they usually have the model's face on the front and up to four of their best photos on the back, some may put up to six images on the back or just use the one photograph on the front (this is especially true for new faces). In this way, it can be seen as a mini-portfolio.

You do not need a Z-card until you have started your professional career, but you may need one if you have decided to go it on your own. These days, your Instagram page could act as your digital Z-card, but it should be curated and specifically tailored to your modeling career.

Established models usually have help from their agent to build their portfolio which just shows how important model agents are in the modeling world. But what's even more important is to choose the right photos and find the right photographers to capture your look. If you don't have the help of an agent, you need to find a good photographer at a reasonable price yourself.

Photoshoots

Finding a photographer

Finding a photographer is relatively easy, but finding a good photographer is hard. When you are looking to find a photographer when you are first starting out you need to thoroughly do your research. You can usually start by googling the type of photographer you are looking for. For example, you could google "fashion photographers" then visit their website to look at their work and reviews.

If you don't know the type of photos you need, a good way to gauge it is to visit modeling agency websites to look through their models and modeling portfolios. Find out what looks you might need and put them together by creating a look-book (a type of mood board for fashion modeling). Once you have done that, you can try to find a photographer that shoots similar photos.

Once you have found your photographer, make sure to do a background check on them, read their Yelp reviews, review on other sites, and check their social media and LinkedIn pages. If you are a minor (under 18), get your parent or guardian to initiate the first call and go with you on the shoot day. Adult models should also take care when meeting strangers for the first time. Do as much background research as possible to make sure the photographer is who they say they are.

Once you have done your research and found the right photographer, the next thing to do is to put your look together and decide what you will wear on the shoot.

Make-up Artist

One person you might need on your shoot is a good make-up artist. Make-up artists are important on modeling shoots because they can help create the look you want and even help improve your skin to shoot better when the light catches it. They sometimes come at an extra cost, but they are worth it if you are shooting with a professional photographer.

Remember that you do not have to organize a professional shoot if you are looking for an agent; they can help you. But if you can't find one and decide to launch your own career, you will need to have some professional photos.

Authenticity: Who are you?

Normally, when working on a modeling job, the stylist puts the looks together. If you do not have a stylist, you should think about the looks you want to have on your shoot. To put looks together, you can use photos from magazines or advertisements that inspire you. Use these to help you get ideas of the looks you want.

For fashion models, the looks are a bit more varied and fashion-oriented. You do not need a lot to put it together. Use magazines to inspire you. A simple tank top, a pair of shorts, and high heels can look amazing once correctly styled and your hair and make-up are done. So, don't worry if you don't have the same outfits as in the magazines.

If you intend to do a commercial shoot, then it's much easier because commercial photos, as mentioned earlier, are for the girl or boy next door, so all you need is casual clothing. Commercial photos are all about personality and showing who you are. Consider a lot of smiles and natural, relaxed looks with nothing over-stylized or overtly extravagant.

Remember that on all shoots, particularly commercial shoots, they want to see who you are. They want to see the real you reflected through your photos. It is important to be authentic and open as you shoot. If you are nervous or anxious, it will show through your photos. It may be worth meeting and interviewing a couple of photographers to make sure you feel comfortable with them before the shoot. This may also help to reduce your anxiety. You can also ask the photographer for their advice and suggestions to make your shoot run smoothly and build a rapport between the both of you.

CHAPTER NINE

Fashion Modeling and Runways

Editorial versus Runway

We talked earlier about the different types of modeling and what each entails. As mentioned, fashion modeling covers both editorial print modeling and runway modeling. Most editorial models are usually also runway models, but not all runway models get a lot of print work.

Runway models

Runway models are also referred to as catwalk models. They are usually tall and thin; designers like to see the clothes hang on a silhouette. Runway models are usually between an American size zero to four or a UK size four to eight. Excessive dieting just to fit into the designer's clothes is not advised for any models or anyone.

There are different types of runway jobs a runway model might get. These could include major designer fashion shows, swimsuit shows, trunk shows run by designers or big department stores, and showroom modeling.

Major designer runway shows

Major designer runway shows take place in London, Paris, New York, and Milan. These include world-renowned designers including Chanel, Dior, Gucci, Versace, and Chloé, to name a few. Other cities have designer shows, too, and smaller designers show all around the world. Department stores sometimes host shows for their customers that span over a few days or a couple of weeks. These are sometimes referred to as trunk shows, and they often take the models from city to city, modeling for the same department store.

Another type of runway modeling is called fit modeling or showroom modeling. Showroom and fit models usually work in-house with the designer. They are sometimes referred to as house models as the designer will get them to try out their new designs or fit them to their body and the model shows the clothes in a smaller, more intimate setting in the designer's showroom or the sales showroom.

There are also different types of showrooms. Some showrooms represent a single designer, while some represent multiple designers. Buyers from various department stores or individually owned stores come in to see the clothes they want to buy for the coming seasons.

Showroom modeling can become a regular gig as most designers show twice a year, and buyers come in to buy, as well, and clients tend to book the same models season after season.

Learning to walk

To be a catwalk model, you have to learn how to walk. I guess you have probably seen models on television, strutting their stuff up and down the catwalk; to be honest, it is not as complicated as it may seem.

A model's walk down the catwalk consists of walking by putting one leg in front of the other and strutting. The way models walk down the runway can change, depending on which designer's clothes they are showing. Normally, designers tell you to have an attitude and personality when walking down the catwalk. Some designers like the models to stroll casually down the catwalk, while others want them to strut. Some shows are on a catwalk podium, and others can be walking around a room. The main thing you should remember is that they love to see your character in your walk. It should be a confident walk, regardless of the walking style.

Different modeling turns

At the end of the catwalk, you will have to do a turn where you turn around and walk back. There are also many different ways of turning on a catwalk. There is the "casual turn," which is similar to strolling. Then there are three-point turns, in which you walk to the front, pose, pose sideways, and swing around.

How to walk depends on the show notes you get before the show starts. You cannot stroll down the catwalk and do a dramatic turn unless required. This is why you are given "show notes" on how to walk by the designer. Each designer likes a different style of walking, and it often depends on their clothing collection.

Your turn has to be in line with your walk. If your walk is extravagant and moody, perhaps a similar turn will work. Watch some fashion shows and observe different modeling style walks and turns. This could be an interesting way to see different walking and turning styles.

Prepping

Before a big runway show starts, there is usually a lot of preparation that takes place backstage. It is not all lights, camera, action. Behind the scenes, there are racks of clothes the models will wear. Each frame is labeled with the model's name and sometimes a photo. There are make-up artists, hairdressers, helpers, and sometimes, even a few press people backstage.

You have to get to the show location a couple of hours before the show to do a quick rehearsal and get ready. First, you are walked through a rehearsal. After rehearsal, you go into hair and make-up. Once finished, you may have to sit around and wait for the show to start. Just before the show starts, you get into your first outfits. The first model to walk down the runway opens the show and the last model out usually closes the show.

Bear in mind that there are other things you should be aware of before walking onto the runway. This includes technical distractions like smoke or mist used to create ambiance or blinding lights. You also need to remember there will be audience members and it may be overwhelming when you walk out in front of such a large crowd of people. Be prepared and don't lose focus. Runway shows are fun so try not to get nervous. Instead, ooze with personality, as you sashay down the runway.

Last but not least, there is a certain etiquette to which you will have to adhere to during a runway show and when prepping. Be careful when posting behind the scenes photos as some designers don't like it, and some models may be in a state of undress. Do not take anything that does not belong to you or ask for free items. If the designer wants to gift things to you, s/he will let you know. Don't invite friends or relatives backstage without permission. You are free to eat and drink as much as you like, provided it does not get in the way of your work. If you don't feel well or do not feel comfortable in something you are asked to wear, let your agent or the designer know.

Editorial shooting

As mentioned earlier, editorial/print models are usually featured in magazines. You may be familiar with some of the more famous models like Bella Hadid, Naomi Campbell, Karli Kloss, Gisele Bundchen, Miranda Kerr, and the list goes on.

In this section, we will talk about what it's like to shoot on an editorial magazine shoot. There are a lot of things to which you have to pay attention. Editorial shoots are a team effort and normally on a shoot, photographers, make-up artists, and hairdressers will be present, and sometimes the client may be present as well. Some editorial shoots may also involve more than one model.

Editorial shoots can be demanding, but models are usually well-taken care of. These shoots will involve you doing different poses or appear in different scenarios on set, so it is best to practice your poses. Be at ease, and let the inner you shine through. Editorial shoots are fun, and you are usually able to view the photos on the photographer's monitor as he/she shoots them. If your shoot is for a magazine, it will usually be released about one to two months after the shoot. It is always flattering to know that thousands of other people from around the world will see you in a magazine.

Bella Hadid

Naomi Campbell

Gisele Bundchen

The Slate

Earlier on, I talked about the slate. The slate, or slating, is for on-camera auditions only. You will be required to state your name and the agent's name that sent you to the audition. You may also be asked to turn around from side to side so they can see both of your profiles. This goes on tape for the casting director's reference. This process is called "slating." Slate tapes are usually sent to the client, so they can see what you like in three-dimensional, real life. Some modeling agencies now use slates so their clients can see what models are like on video. It is a good idea as it lets you show off your personality.

Castings

A casting is an appointment to meet a client for the first time. Usually, when you go to a casting, there are several other models from different agencies present. You will have to wait your turn, and then you go in to see the casting director or client. The client typically looks through your portfolio, asks you questions about yourself, and they may, occasionally, tell you to try on a garment or take a quick snapshot, depending on what the casting is for. If the client is casting for a runway show, they may tell you to give them a walk or ask you what other major runway shows you have done. If they are interested in booking you, they will let your agent know.

Go-sees are similar to castings but are more like a meet and greet situation in which you go in to see the client, and they say hello and get to meet you. These meetings are good because they help the client get familiar with you and meet you for the first time, especially if you are a new face.

Before we go on, I would like to talk about a couple of things.

Successful models are usually very busy, and there are certain things to which you should always pay attention. We will go through them individually. Some of them are lifestyle choices, while others just have to do with the day-to-day of being a model.

Weight

Your weight is important if you are a fashion or runway model as they are generally quite slim and slender. So, if you tend to put on weight, it is advisable to maintain a well-balanced diet and exercise regularly. I don't advise anyone to go on a full-time or drastic weight loss diet as this is too extreme. The good news is that models today can be healthy. Some models were required to be drastically thin in the past, but those days are now over, and the norm is to just be slim, or at least trim. You can easily do this by taking up some exercises at the gym and eating healthily.

Skincare

Good skincare is essential. Models should have good skin, and a good skincare routine is necessary. To maintain good skin, make sure you wash off all make-up, use a toner, a good moisturizer, and do not over-tan. If you are dealing with acne or spots, try to see a dermatologist. Good skin is essential if you want to be a model, as photographers will want to photograph you and make sure your skin looks amazing.

Hygiene

Hygiene is another important factor. Always be sure to practice good personal hygiene.

Mental / Spiritual health

Modeling can sometimes take a toll on you as there is a lot of rejection involved. Make sure you are mentally stable and don't take things personally. If a client does not book you for a job, it usually does not have anything to do with you. Sometimes, you just don't have the look, they are looking for that's all. You have to find peace knowing that you may have to go through a lot of castings to get a single booking. Be patient, and eventually, you will get booked.

Relationships in real life, with fans, online, and love interests

As your modeling career develops, there is a chance you may become popular, either on social media or in real life. When this happens, you will have many fans and admirers who may send you messages and gifts. This can be overwhelming at worst and flattering at best, but you must always exercise safety and precaution.

If you are on social media, you can message fans back if you want to, but keep it at that. Never give fans or people you don't know your home address. Don't plan to meet them, especially if you do not go with a parent or guardian. Be wary of people sending you gifts or clients contacting you through social media asking to meet up with you. Refer both of these situations to your agent. Gifts can be accepted, of course, but only through your agent or manager.

Be careful of frauds and other online scammers posing as regular people. If someone sends you messages that may be considered rude, offensive, or threatening, you can block them and report them to the local authorities.

Try to keep your day to day life as normal as possible. Modeling is a job, so treat it as one, and don't get hooked on all the trappings of the fashion industry. Most importantly, remember your safety is paramount, so please stay safe.

C H A P T E R   T E N

The Big Four

Four main cities are the epicenters of the fashion modeling industry worldwide. These are London, Paris, New York, and Milan. These are the main designers' shows; any fashion designer who wants to be in the mainstream fashion has to show in one of these four cities.

The most important city of the four is Paris. Paris Fashion Week is a series of designer presentations held biannually in Paris, France, with spring/summer and autumn/winter events held each year. The schedule begins with New York, followed by London, and then Milan, and ends in Paris. I would personally say that Milan Fashion Week comes in a close second to Paris.

A fashion week consists of a week of organized events with multiple designer collections. Before this organized event was recognized in New York City, fashion showings were held in Paris as early as the 1700s. These early showings were only for clients purchasing items, that were displayed on mannequins. In the 1800s, showings began to change. Charles Frederick Worth began showing multiple pieces together and with a higher design. Jeanne Paquin was the first designer to make her showings public, and Paul Poiret was the first to host parties after his events.

In addition to ready-to-wear shows, there are men's and haute couture shows held semi-annually for the spring/summer and autumn/winter seasons. Every year, famous brands like Dior, Chanel, Louis Vuitton, Givenchy, and Céline host their shows in historical places such as the Carrousel du Louvre and the Grand Palais.

Milan Fashion Week

Milan Fashion Week is a clothing trade show held semi-annually in Milan, Italy. The autumn/winter event is held in February/March of each year, and the spring/summer event is held in September/October of each year. It is partially organized by Camera Nazionale della Moda Italiana (The National Chamber for Italian Fashion), a non-profit association that disciplines, coordinates, and promotes Italian fashion development and is responsible for hosting fashion events and shows in Milan.

New York Fashion Week

New York Fashion Week, held in February and September of each year, is a semi-annual series of events where international fashion collections are shown to buyers, the press, and the general public.

It is one of four major fashion weeks globally, collectively known as the "Big Four," along with those in Paris, London, and Milan. The Council of Fashion Designers of America created the modern notion of a centralized "New York Fashion Week" in 1993. However, cities like London were already using their cities' names in conjunction with the words Fashion Week in the 1980s. New York Fashion Week is based on a much older series of events called "Press Week," founded in 1943. It has consisted of numerous branded events, such as Olympus Fashion Week, New York, MADE Fashion Week, and many independent fashion productions around town.

London Fashion Week

London Fashion Week is a clothing trade show that takes place in London twice a year, in February and September. The event showcases over 250 designers to a global audience of influential media and retailers. It is organized by the British Fashion Council for the London Development Agency with help from the Department for Business, Innovation, and Skills, London Fashion Week first took place in October 1983.

Over five thousand press and buyers attend London Fashion Week which generates over £100 million in orders at every event. A retail-focused event, London Fashion Week Festival, takes place immediately afterward at the same venue and is open to the general public.

You may wonder how you might get to work in all of these markets, and if you have to travel to all of these countries. There are modeling agents worldwide in several categories but in high fashion modeling, the same models travel all over the world to all of the markets to work in these big fashion shows.

Normally, after you join a fashion modeling agency, if they think you are great for runway shows, the agent might start to get you some work in your hometown. If s/he wants you to get more work in print or on the runway, they usually send your materials to other agencies worldwide. These worldwide agencies then contact your agency if they are interested in representing you. Sometimes, they will advance your flight and accommodation expenses and take them out of your next paycheck.

When you go to a new city through your agent, the agency that sends you to the new city is described as your "mother agency." They represent you and ensure that the new agency you will work with pays you and takes care of you. It might also get a small commission from the other agency when you work. You can decide to change your mother agency at any time. Some agents have exclusive contracts with their clients to prevent them from changing agencies, but you can usually get out of such agreements with a good attorney.

There are things you should also bear in mind when going to work abroad or in another city. Make sure to practice safety. Do not meet with strangers in remote places. Always tell your agent, your parents, or the authorities if you have any issues. If you don't like anything about your agency or agents, report it to your mother agency. You can also try to change agencies while abroad. I would also like to say here, that if you find an agency in a different country and don't have an agency in your hometown. If you decide to travel to another place or country to join that agency, please check them out properly before traveling to sign with them. You have to be sure that they are an actual business doing what they say they do, representing models.

You will meet other models while working abroad, and they tend to be supportive, and all want to build friendships. That said, modeling abroad can be lonely at times as you may have to go to castings by yourself, and you may be living by yourself too.

As I mentioned before, modeling can provide a world of opportunity, especially for fashion models willing to travel to different cities. This is a great perk of the job.

CHAPTER ELEVEN

Teen Modeling

One can start modeling at any age, but anyone under legal adult age must be accompanied by a parent or guardian, especially when joining an agency. In commercial modeling, models start very young. Even a baby can be a commercial model, as they are used in commercial print advertisements and on television.

If you have been signed as a child, your agent will usually give you advice as you grow older as to whether you should go down the fashion or commercial route. Fashion models usually start around age fifteen, whereas commercial models can start at any age. If you were a commercial model as a child but moved toward fashion as you grew older, your agent will guide you and help you find a fashion agency if they don't represent fashion models.

Once you start adult modeling, you may be asked to shoot adult clothes, and you will have hair and make-up done in an older style. As you have already had modeling experience, the transition into this type of modeling may be easier than for those with no modeling experience.

If you are in school, try to stay in education and model part-time while you finish college. If you decide to model as a teen, try to go back to college once you are in your early twenties. Modeling as a career is not guaranteed, so it is better to complete your education, so you always have a back-up plan.

I must emphasize that modeling can be a very competitive profession, and only a few are guaranteed to even make any money from it, so bear this in mind.

Your right to privacy

I would like to talk about your right to privacy, labor laws, and child protection issues.

First, let's talk about privacy. Even as a model, you have a right to privacy whenever you shoot or make a video. The images belong to the client but you have to sign a release so they can use them, and you are, of course, compensated for this. Photos of you in a state of undress or when you are backstage cannot be released to the public without your consent.

Your health information has to be kept private by the agency, as well as any personal information the agent may know or have about your personal life. You also have the right not to divulge any information about yourself that is not related to modeling or any job you do. Again, if you feel uncomfortable about anything, report it to your agent or legal guardian immediately.

Labor laws for minors

There are different labor laws for minors, depending on the city, state, or country in which you work. These laws differ by state and by city and country. Child labor laws can usually be found by contacting your local labor department or a google search. Labor laws usually state how long a child can work each day if s/he is on-set or any other work situation. There are also regulations concerning schooling and taking classes. Adult guardians or parents should be with the child or minor on-set all of the time. This rule applies in most countries, and it is there for your safety and security.

We have talked about starting a modeling career and what it takes to be successful in this career. As mentioned earlier, you can model commercially at any age. But with fashion modeling, you can only model when you reach the approximate age of fifteen as the work is focused on modeling adult clothes.

To summarize, you don't necessarily need an agent, if you're just starting out, you can use your social media as a digital portfolio and source work yourself. Modeling is a subjective profession, so you have to be thick-skinned. It will involve rejection at times as you will not book every job you go out for, you have to stay positive and focused.

I am sure that with the right amount of determination and the road map this book has given you, you will most likely succeed exponentially in your modeling career.

CHAPTER TWELVE

Top Tips

Audition hacks

As you may know or have come to realize, modeling is a people-oriented business. People hire people they like, or they hire friends of theirs, so good relationships are everything in the modeling world. You have to maintain good relationships, which may pay off in the long run. When you meet potential clients for the first time, not only are they looking to see if you are the type of model they need for the job, but they also judge how easy you will be to work with. So be sure to be likable and respectful and remember, first impressions count.

Below are a few hacks I have discovered that could increase your chances of booking jobs and getting ahead of the competition.

Behavior

Due to the nature of this job, you will end up meeting a lot of people from different walks of life, different races, ethnicities, genders, and ages. Remember that there is no space in the modeling industry for negative comments about race, sexuality, or gender. If you feel like someone is being discriminatory, make it known, and let your agent know. When you meet new people in the modeling industry, be kind, cordial, and behave appropriately. Be respectful on shoots and locations.

Personality wins

As mentioned previously, when you meet with a client or an agent, your personality counts for a lot. Clients and agents want to be sure that you are easy to work with and that you will not be a prima donna or egotistical when working with you. My advice to you is always to be polite and friendly. If a client annoys you report the incident to your agent or the appropriate authorities. You do not have to pick a fight.

Remember that the modeling world is small, and people talk a lot (and unfortunately, a lot of them talk a lot of shit), so creating a toxic working situation could backfire on you. Being polite and having a positive outlook does not, however, mean that you should let people walk all over you. Always handle your business cordially, even when it annoys you.

Timekeeping

When it comes to castings and auditions, always be sure you get there on time or early. The advantage of getting to your appointment early is that often none of the other models are there yet. When you show up first, you may get to meet the client before they get busy with other models. You could have time to talk and create a rapport with them. This can help create a connection between you and the client, and even if they don't book you for that job, they will remember you. Remember that the client is a human being, just like you.

I always advise models to look-up the location they will be shooting the night before the shoot. Find the location on Google and plan your trip. If you are going to use public transportation, check train and bus times, and allow yourself at least 20 minutes extra time in case of detours along the way. Most model shoots start early in the morning, so you might be able to avoid traffic and congestion. Once you get to the shoot, sign in with the assistant or whoever is in charge of signing in models. If the location is far afield, sometimes the client will send you a car to pick-up. Let your agency know when you arrive and when you leave the set to go home.

So, always remember to never be late for an audition. Tardiness does not serve you, nor will it benefit your reputation. Being late may delay the whole shoot, and the client might be paying millions just to use the location. If you have to be late, let your agent or manager know so they can call the client ahead of time and inform them that you are running late.

Clean, clean, clean

When it comes to modeling, always remember that, as a model, you are a canvas that the client uses to advertise their wares. Clients need to see your naked skin and the real you. They want to see your face, your bone structure, and they want to make sure that your skin is nice, clean, fresh, and looks good. Do not go in to meet clients or agents with excessive make-up and hair extensions. Clients want to see models in a natural and clean state. They want to see you—they do not want to see a version of you. Even if they end up putting excessive make-up and glamorous clothing on you, they do not expect you to arrive for auditions with all of the make-up and clothing. Keep it simple. Do not be excessive. Just present yourself simply, and you will be fine.

Build connections

It may sound like I am repeating myself, but I will say it again: try and build connections with clients, stylists, make-up artists, and agents. It is important to treat them like friends, but at the same time, be professional.

There are several ways you can build connections in a conversation. Ask them about their kids, their families, or their work. You do not need to delve too deeply, but at least be interested in who they are. This helps you build connections with them on a deeper level. Remember that people love working with people they like. If they like you, they will want to work with you again in the future.

Personality always wins. Smile and be nice. Modeling is a long-term career, so being nice and accessible goes a long way.

Agency hacks

Unless you are lucky enough to have already signed with an agency, finding a good modeling agency can be tough. Most agencies have open-calls whereas others ask you to send your photos and information by mail. Agents receive several thousand submissions daily, and sometimes, standing out among all of the other models can be kind of hard to accomplish. If you are trying to find an agent, below are a few hacks that could help you immensely when it comes to getting your foot in the door.

Research

Before approaching agents, a rule of thumb is to always go to their website to see if they have anyone else that looks similar to you. By doing this, you can establish the type of talent they represent and what kind of look they favor. You can see if you fit into their niche and if they will be the right representation for you. Another good insight you can get from an agency's website is the clients their models work with. It can give you an edge if you know their clients, as you may be able to get a recommendation from one of them with a little-known trick I am about to show you.

Be knowledgeable

When you meet an agent, it is best to go in prepared. Know a bit about the agency and the modeling industry. You do not need to know more than is necessary, but having good knowledge of the agency is a bonus and shows that you take your work seriously.

Get recommendations

Agents need clients to book models—that's how they make their money. Without clients booking models, the agencies cannot make an income. If you can get a client to recommend you to an agency, you stand a better chance of the agency representing you, so that's a big bonus. This is a hack that some models have used in the past.

It is usually easier to sign on to an agency with references rather than find representation by yourself. This simple hack may help you get the recommendation you need. It may be difficult to find out what clients agencies are affiliated with or which clients have booked models through that agent, so you may need to do a bit of research. One way is to look at the modeling agency's website to see the models' portfolios. Once you see a few of the clients their models have worked with, you can call the clients to find out which department books models and get key contact names.

WARNING: THIS HACK IS RISKY

Once you find out the name of the person who books models in that department, you can call the agency, pretending to be the client's assistant, and say that you would like for them to see a model you recently met and who you think would be a good fit with their agency.

It may be better to get a friend to do the calling so your voice won't be the same when you turn up to the agency. Just say to the agency that you have met a model you think they should see, and you would like to recommend him/her. Give the model's name and tell them that the model will call. Wait for a couple of days, call the agency as yourself, and say that you would like to come in for a meeting and that a client recommended you. Give the client's name. The agency will most likely be delighted that you called, and when you go in for an appointment or open-call, you will get special attention. Being recommended by a client means that you stand a good chance of being booked.

Remember that this hack should be used in moderation. Make sure that you follow the instructions carefully, and don't call clients that don't book models with your look, as when you go in to see the modeling agency, they will easily find out. Also, make sure you know a bit about the client. You do not want to pretend you are the client's assistant on the phone only to find out they don't have one.

Another good place to get recommendations for agencies is through the photographers that agents work with. Again, once you have found a photographer with whom the agency regularly works, perhaps you can book a shoot with that photographer. On the shoot, be friendly and likable. The photographer will probably ask you if you already have representation. If you say you don't, they may refer you to one of the agencies they frequently work with if they think you are a good fit. As I mentioned previously, modeling is a people's business. If someone likes you and thinks you are right for a particular agency, they will most likely recommend you to that agency.

Target them

If all else fails and you do not get an agent, keep trying. Meet with all of the good agencies in your city. If they don't work out, give it a month or two, and try again. If you can't find an agent, this should not stop you. In this day and age, with the Internet and all that, you can just go out there and do your own thing. There are several platforms and social media apps, as well as alternate ways to get yourself seen. Perseverance always pays off in the end, so don't give up. Stay focused on your end goal, and you will eventually find the right agent to represent you. It may take one or two tries, but you can eventually break in if you keep trying.

Below are some ways you can build influence and get agents and clients to notice you. Remember that having a modeling agency does not necessarily guarantee an income. In this career, you always have to try to get work for yourself. Agents are only there to help partially facilitate the process.

Influence

The modeling industry has grown, and with the exponential growth of the industry, models market themselves as mega-brands, and clients are booking them to help promote their brands. In today's world, you can maintain your top place as a model easier if you establish a brand.

Many models have become mega-brands, such as the likes of Giselle Bundchen, Kate Moss, and Kendall Jenner. Today's designers sometimes like using models that are already famous as it gets their brands further exposure. That being said, you can start building your own brand identity even without a modeling agent. If you don't find a modeling agent, you may still attract clients because your brand has already been well-built, which will be beneficial to them.

Today, building a brand and getting exposure has never been easier because there are various platforms, including social media platforms, where you can build a digital portfolio and interact with future clients and the general public.

Let's talk about some social media platforms and modeling platforms that may be useful in helping you achieve your success. As mentioned earlier in this book, you need to carefully curate your photos and make sure your photos are professional. Still, the great thing about social media is that you can mix it with some personal photos and images. Brands want to see who you are authentically.

CHAPTER THIRTEEN

Touchy Subjects

I decided to write this chapter because I want to bring up a few topics that people avoid talking about in the fashion industry. These topics may be touchy, but they are the truth of this industry. Like real life, the fashion industry is full of good and bad people, and it is up to you to make the right decisions. I will attempt to cover all of these touchy subjects in-depth to give more perspective on how you can avoid falling victim to any of these pitfalls.

Remember that you can always say no and walk away from any situation. You do not have to trade your soul for booking a job.

Money management

One thing agents don't talk about to models is how to manage their money. Model agents are notorious for having various hidden fees and overcharging models. Most models do not have any financial education and often get ripped off by agencies. An example of this is agents charge models 5%+ to advance money after a job. The billing cycle for the client is 30 days but it can take up to 60 days. Sometimes the model needs money to live so they take an advance from the agency, and the agency charges a fee.

Some agents have been found to have already been paid by the client yet they still invoice the model exorbitant fees for an advance. Agents have also been known to mismanage their models' funds. Some agents run an account for the model on their books and invoice the model for everything. So they may book flights, pay rent, and expenses for the model and bill them later. The agencies do not necessarily try and find the best deals for the model, especially if she is making a lot of money they book whatever they think the model may like or deserve.

The thing here is that you could be making thousands, and your agency is spending it on your behalf without you even keeping track of what is being spent. This is very dangerous as by the time you come in to get your funds, the agency will produce a list of expenses and you may have hardly anything left. Models have to be financially savvy. You work hard to make money so you cannot let anyone take advantage of your lack of financial know-how.

I would advise you to get some financial education. There are lots of online resources out there that you can use. In today's world, you can pay as little as $11.99 on Udemy to learn a bit about finances. The truth of the matter is that many models end up broke due to a lack of financial education and money management. Agents know this, and the bad ones take advantage.

It is a good idea if you are young to have a mentor that helps you plan financially. Yes, modeling can be very lucrative, but first-class flights can also be very expensive. The agency will assume you want a first-class flight if you are making tons of money, so they will book you one. Meanwhile, you may have been able to use your sky miles and fly premium economy for half the price.

In the modeling high fashion industry, you are practically finished as soon as you are twenty-six unless you are a breakout star or a brand. So, be sure to learn how to manage your money.

Education

Now let's talk about education. Most models start rather young and get disrupted from school as their career requires them to start young. I want to emphasize that a good 70% of models will never make a full-time living from modeling, so it is smart to start thinking of what you want to do either after your career is over or whilst you are modeling.

Some models have part-time jobs but focus mostly on modeling as they are hoping to "make it" one day. My advice to you is, don't sweat it. There will be a lot of time so use it wisely. Again, the good news today is that you can get a study online. Find something you love and get good at it so if all else fails you have something to fall back on.

Nothing is set in stone in the world of modeling, so don't let time fly. Use your youth wisely. Follow your modeling dreams, but at the same time, don't lose your ambition to do the things you have to do in life. Time flies and things change so be prepared to change with it. Get a skill aside from modeling as you may need to rely on it if things don't work out. If you can't afford college, then start some online courses. It is of utmost importance. Your future depends on this.

Race and prejudice

This is a subject that a lot of people like to avoid. When I was modeling full-time, racism existed in plain sight. The industry was prejudice against models of color; the discrimination against black models at the time was just out of this world.

Below is a story I was told by my good friend Karen Muld who was one of the most successful models of her time:

"One of my best friends and mentors was a black model named Katusha, who went on to become one of the most successful runway models in the world. Way back, we used to hang out and go on castings together, but she would not get as many castings as I did. Sometimes, our agent would send black models to castings that were general open-calls for all models. I remember that in one situation, in particular, Katusha and I arrived, and as soon as the client saw Katusha, I saw his attitude change. He looked through my model portfolio, and when it was Katusha's turn, he just looked at the first page, closed her portfolio, and said, "Give me a minute." We saw him go into his office, and through the glass window, we saw him pick up the phone. He had called the agency, and we heard him say, "I told you not to send black models!"

I could not believe what I had heard. How could that man say that right in front of us? How dare he say that to the agency?"

The truth was that these agencies knew about the racism going on in the industry, but there was not much they could do about it as they depended on these clients to book their models. There was and still is prejudice on the runway. Sometimes designers would not use models of color in their runway shows, and when they did, they would say things like, "There is only space for one black model on my runway," while they would book twenty or more Caucasian models.

Agents and agencies allowed this to happen, though many of them tried to help models of color by representing them and forcing clients to see them. However, because of the lack of work for models of color, most agencies only represented a handful. Basically, for every fifty white models an agency represented, they would represent one model of color.

There was space for only one Black model at the top, and at the time, it was Naomi Campbell, and she was not about to let in any other black models because the competition was fierce at the time. Naomi Campbell is well-known for having a confrontation with Tyra Banks, another black model, mainly because she saw her as competition. There is a famous episode of the "Tyra Banks Show," where she confronts Naomi Campbell years later. Naomi Campbell denies this accusation and has turned into an advocate for giving black models opportunity on the runway.

Things have changed a lot since then, markets are more receptive to models of color now. Clients are much more open and willing to use all races and nationalities – they want to be inclusive, and are. Many models of color are blazing the way forward on the modeling and runway scene including Alek Wek, Liya Kadebe, Maria Borges, Cindy Bruna, Jordan Dunn, and Jazmeen Tookes.

Even though things have moved forward, elements of racism and prejudice remain. There are still not enough opportunities out there for models of color and you may often feel as if you are being judged by your color and not by your talent. If you get to work on a job, meet an agency or client, and you feel as if they are racist or prejudiced toward you, kindly make it known. This should not happen, period! Let your parents, agent, manager, or guardian know. If you are being harassed, call the authorities.

Karen Mulder

Tyra Banks

CHAPTER FOURTEEN

Nepotism

Nepotism, a form of favoritism that is granted to relatives or friends, exists in every field, but it is highly prevalent in the modeling industry. Many of the world's top models including Kaia Gerber, Kate Moss, Adwoa Aboah, Gigi Hadid, Bella Hadid, Kendall Jenner, Cara Delevingne, Poppy Delevingne, and many more celebrity kids, rose to fame on the backs of their parents' connections.

Adwoa Aboah is the daughter of Camilla Lowther, who runs one of the world's most successful artist management agencies. CLM is an artist management agency based in London and New York, representing photographers, directors, stylists, art directors, makeup artists, and hairstylists. It only makes sense that the daughter of the owner would become a top model, even though she is not a normal model standard as she is shorter than normal but has a great face and personality.

Let's talk about Kaia Gerber, Cindy Crawford's daughter. Fortunately for her, she has her mother's face, she looks good, and she has a great body. She is a great model, but her mum being a famous model, definitely helped. Kendall Jenner only became a successful model because of her family name, but fortunately, Kendall has a great body, good bone structure, and very disciplined. Still, her family's connections guaranteed her success and helped her get to the top.

Lily-Rose, the daughter of Johnny Depp and French actress Vanessa Paradis. Lily-Rose is also on the shorter side (like her mother), a Chanel model and a famous actress in France. Lily-Rose, due to being the daughter of Vanessa Paradis and Johnny Depp, rose to the top of the Paris fashion scene.

Another such example is Anwar Hadid, whose sisters are Bella and Gigi Hadid. They became famous because of their father, Mohamed Hadid, and their mom Yolanda Hadid who was married to David Foster, a mega-famous music producer, composer, and executive.

You start to realize that nepotism is a common occurrence in the modeling industry. That said, nepotism is also rampant in many industries, and in countries like the United Kingdom, nepotism is part of the system in general.

The reason I'm telling you this is so that you do not get disheartened when you've been trying to get an agent, and you realize that somebody who is a celebrity's daughter or son is all of a sudden on the cover of a magazine.

The result of nepotism is obvious, when models whose parents are famous, photographers, agents, managers, stylists, or makeup artists become top models. Their parents are friends with other leading photographers and image-makers in the industry, and they help them stay and get to the top. A classic case of people helping people they like.

Nepotism is rife in every field and in modeling nepotism happens on every level. Make sure to put yourself forward and be ahead of

Cindy Crawford

Gigi Hadid

your peers, these simple tricks and tips we have talked about will help you rise slightly above the others in the game. I mean your family is probably not famous, your parents are not super-rich, you are not the cousin of the editor of Vogue, and you're not friends with a famous photographer. That's why you have to be professional as stated in this book and use some of the hacks I talk about earlier to pave your way forward.

If you're polite, professional, meet the modeling industry's standards, and have a good work ethic, you will most likely end up getting work anyway. So, don't stress yourself about models that use their connections to rise to the top. But remember modeling is a tough profession, and you need grit, discipline, and a lot of energy to keep yourself at the top.

CHAPTER FIFTEEN

The Pitfalls of the Modeling Industry

Sexual advances

Modeling is an industry where there are a lot of very pretty women and very handsome men. After all, looks matter a lot in the modeling industry. Models often find themselves constantly being hit-on by clients, photographers, and agents, the very people who are supposed to be taking care of and protecting them. I am not saying that this happens every day, but you have to be aware of this. A fair number of models get sucked up into this, thinking it will be advantageous to their careers in the future. Some models even provide sexual services to get work. My advice is to never give any of yourself away because you're trying to get a job. There are enough modeling jobs out there so you do not have to sell your body, soul, or any part of yourself just because you want to get to the top.

Beware! Many users in the modeling industry will try to use young talents for their benefit. Let me give you an example: When you travel worldwide as a model, you will live in "model apartments" or "model hotels". Model apartments and model hotels are usually long-term, temporary accommodations at which the model can stay while working in the city. It can be fun staying in a model apartment because you get to meet other models, have fun going to castings together, go out together in the evenings, work out together, and make friends. But some model apartments are cramped and sleep two models in a room while charging each model the price of the whole apartment. Model apartments can be uncomfortable because you may not get on with your fellow models.

Model apartments and hotels are notorious for having strange people hang around. When I say that people hang around, I mean promoters (guys who are basically pimps) who disguise themselves as club promoters and promise to take models out for dinners and nightclubs for free, in exchange for them going out for the night to have a good time. When these promoters first preposition you, they make it seem like they are saying, "Come out with us tonight. You're going to have a good time. We're going to get you a free dinner, and you can bring all of your other model friends." I'm not saying it's not fun — it usually is fun. They typically grab a bunch of models (usually eight to ten or more) and organize a car to take you to dinner at a nice restaurant where you have free food. After that, it is straight to a nightclub where you get VIP entrance, a table is waiting for you with a lot of alcohol to drink and you can party all night. Sounds like fun, right?

What some models don't realize is that these promoters are paid to bring you to the restaurants and nightclubs. They are getting paid because they believe that by having pretty women and maybe a few handsome guys at a venue, they will attract more customers, to the restaurant or the nightclub. These venues pay the promoter to go scouting for pretty girls and bring them to the lounge or the restaurant to have dinner and take them dancing. Sounds fun, doesn't it?

Now, I'm not saying that you shouldn't go nightclubbing. I am saying that nightclubbing and dining out can be a lot of fun, especially when you're doing it with your girlfriends or the male friends you made in the models' apartment. You have to be aware that these promoters promise to take care of the models, make sure they have a good time, and get them home safely, some of them keep that promise, but a lot of them don't. Promoters take the models to the nightclubs and offer them drinks and stuff, but many of these girls are usually young, and it is often the first time in their lives that they have been exposed to an atmosphere with alcohol, drugs, and suspicious gentlemen hanging around.

Drugs

Modeling can be a fun, adventurous job and provide many, many opportunities. You get to attend parties, meet celebrities, heads of states, and heads of companies, and go to places and countries you never imagined visiting. This lifestyle may seem glamorous, but like everything else in life, you have to look out for the pitfalls of the profession. Hidden behind the glamorous parties, the catwalk shows, the movie premieres, and all of the lavish parties is a world of debauchery.

As with the entertainment and music industries, many recreational drugs are floating about in the fashion world. Models have been known to go to parties and take cocaine, ecstasy, and other drug concoctions. I know that people may ask why I am talking about this in a modeling book, but I think this is important and is something you should be aware of so you can avoid it. I would advise any young model who is starting in the industry to be aware and not accept any drugs, recreational or otherwise, from anybody. If you are ever offered any of these drugs, please let your guardian know or call the authorities.

In the past, many models have been addicted to drugs which had detrimental effects on their lives. In the 1980s, famous model Gia, became addicted to heroin which ruined her career and she eventually died of a drug overdose. In the early 2000s, models including Naomi Campbell and Kate Moss also had incidents of drug-taking. So, please be aware of party promoters, agents, or clients who offer you any recreational drugs, and please let somebody know about this. Models can use social media or other digital resources to get their stories told and expose any culprits if need be.

As mentioned several times in this book, professionalism is the number one thing you have, followed by discipline, good character, and preparation. Avoid drugs at any cost, even if you're offered them by someone you think is a good friend.

Diet

Now, let's go on to the subject of diet. Everyone thinks that models are always dieting because they are thin, but many models don't do extreme dieting. They look skinny because they have naturally small bones and a small, thin, petite frame, even though they are tall. When I was a model, I used to say that fashion models look like aliens because of our tall stature and small bones that make us look so gangly and waif-like.

Back when I was a model, we were told to diet so our hip measurements wouldn't be larger than 34 inches. Nowadays, models don't have to be super-thin or super-gangly to be booked or signed to an agency. Even couture models who used to be extremely thin are curvier than they used to be.

As a model, especially if you are a runway model, you have to have a thin figure, but you do not have to diet excessively. If you're a little overweight, you can do physical exercise, go to the gym, and eat three moderate, calorie-counted meals a day. In my day, the gym was not part of a model's routine. Most models just wanted to be skinny, and there were situations in which models would eat oranges all day or eat cotton wool to fill their stomachs without eating calories. So please do not extreme diet as it will deprive you of food and damage your health.

If an agent tells you to diet excessively or s/he tells you that you are not good enough, it might be best if you leave that agent to find one who can represent you as you are. As mentioned before, runway fashion models have to be thin because the thin silhouette is what designers look for. These models are usually skinny because they have been blessed genetically with a particular body proportion and frame which is why they look so thin.

My advice to you is that you should look into other modeling types if you're struggling with body weight. There are so many modeling jobs for plus-size models and curvy girls, including swimsuit modeling, catalog modeling, and a vast array of commercial modeling.

Remember that you do not have to injure your body or deprive yourself of three square meals a day or nutrition to be a model. Becoming anorexic or bulimic can not only ruin your health, but it can shorten your lifespan. There's always a model agent who will represent you just the way you are.

The Model's Success Workbook

Throughout this book, I have talked about many things you have to do as a model. I have given you practical tips, solutions, and knowledge that I have learned throughout the years of being a top model myself. I hope that you apply these to your career and use this knowledge to help you further your career and rise above the rest.

Now, I could not end this book without giving you some tips. I want to provide you with a model's success roadmap of the things you should do daily to further your career as a model.

That being said, I'm going to give you a few tips. Start a model workbook that you can use to track your modeling career. The first thing we're going to talk about is the measurement card.

Measurement card

As mentioned in earlier chapters of this book, most professional models carry around what is called a Z-card when they go to an audition. The Z-card lists the model's measurements and height and has two to eight pictures. Some agencies have two photos on the Z-card, and other agencies have up to eight pictures on the Z-card.

If you haven't found an agent yet, I don't advise investing in a Z-card, but you should know your measurements. So, instead, I urge you to create a little card or have a word document where you write out the following measurements. You should know these measurements, and you should have them on hand if an agent, client, or photographer wants to book you asks what your measurements are.

Below are the measurements that should be on your Z-card for male and female models:

Women	Men
Dress Size	Pant Size
Height	Height
Weight	Weight
Bust Size	Shoulder Size
Waist	Waist
Hips	Shoe Size
Shoe Size	In-seam
In-seam	

Buy yourself a measuring tape, preferably one that has both inches and centimeters. Use this tape to take your measurements. You can get a friend, guardian, or someone you know to help you. Take these measurements and write them down, so you know what they are, and memorize them.

Type of modeling you want to achieve

Another thing you should be thinking about is the type of modeling you want to do and the type of modeling for which your body-type is suited. As mentioned, if you want to be a runway fashion model, you have to be at least five-foot-nine inches tall. Sometimes you can be slightly shorter, but agents will rarely sign-up girls who are less than five-foot-nine or five-foot-eight-and-a-half for a runway. Apart from that, if you want to be a runway fashion model, you have to be thin and gangly, not necessarily skinny, but you stand a better chance if you have an elongated body. As you now know, fashion modeling is not the only type of modeling, even though it is the one that we see most often because these models are in magazines all the time.

There are other types of modeling, including commercial, plus-size, sports, swimsuit, hand, and foot modeling, the list goes on. The only difference is that there isn't as much work as if you were a commercial model or a fashion model in certain categories of modeling. It is good to know which category you fit in before you embark on a modeling career. You do not want to be one type of model trying to fit into another modeling type. That would be like trying to fit a square peg into a round hole. I advise every model to know and study the type of modeling they think they can do or the category they would fit.

To find out what type of modeling you can do, you should look through magazines and catalogs for inspiration. When you see people who look like you or have your body type, it can help to give you an idea of the kind of modeling you might do. You can also go to modeling agencies and look at their websites, the Internet, or Instagram, to see which category you fit into.

Photos

Photographs are as important as a diploma or college degree when you are looking for a job. Your photos are the first things clients will look at before deciding to book you or use you in a job. I give a lot of tips on finding photographers in your district, area, state, city, or country.

You can do a simple Google search, and once you find some photographers, you can go through their online portfolios. If this is the case, you can see who they have worked with and do a bit of research about the photographer. You can ask a parent or guardian to help you look for photographers and organize a photoshoot.

If you cannot afford a photoshoot, don't worry about it. Get a friend with a good camera to help you take some photos. If you don't have a friend with camera skills, take some pictures yourself. Modeling agents are not worried about having professional photographs. They are more interested in seeing clean, natural photos, and once they see you, they will know what they can do with you.

These people are professionals who have been working in the industry for years and years. They have a very good eye and pay attention to detail, so don't worry about the photos if you don't have a photographer or cannot afford one. Just take some nice pictures with your digital camera.

I know that many young people are very good with editing apps in today's world, so even if you take a picture and the lighting isn't good enough, you can brighten the image to make it look nice. As I mentioned earlier, if you can't get an agent, it's time to start curating your own Instagram page.

Go to agency open-calls

When it is time to start thinking about finding a modeling agency, you can send your photos to them by mail. You can also go on open-calls, and if you go on an open-call and they don't take you on, make a note of it, and ask the person who is doing the open-call why you're not right for them, and they will tell you why they don't think you're a good fit for their agency. If you're not a good fit for them, they will sometimes recommend another agency that you might be a better fit for.

A good thing about going to agency open-calls is that it also allows you to see the competition. You'll be able to see other models who are also trying to get agents and some models who have already signed with the agency. Agencies look for character, as well as the obvious. They want to see how personable you are because that is sometimes what makes clients book one model over another.

We have talked about photos, agencies, and your card measurements. The next thing I want to talk about is discipline. If you're going to find a modeling agency and get representation, you will need to be disciplined in the process of finding one.

Discipline

Set up a schedule of how you're going to call the agencies every week to find out their open-call times. Make a list of agents to whom you sent your photos, which ones you still have to send your photos to, and the ones that have said no. Re-target them again in a few months if they have said no. Sometimes an agency will say no because they already have another model that looks similar, but in the future, they might say yes, so don't give up hope of signing with that particular modeling agency.

This is like any other job. It can be a bit of hard work, but if you push, you will eventually get an agent.

Conclusion

As in life, every good thing must come to an end, and this is where I am going to end this book. I have attached a list of modeling agencies from all of the world's main cities, including London, Paris, Milan, New York, Cape Town, Los Angeles, Chicago, Miami, Athens, Singapore, Hong Kong, and Madrid. These are the main modeling cities, but don't forget that there are modeling agencies in every single city globally, and all you need to do is search for them on Google. Let Google be your best friend.

There are two things that I would like to mention before I end this book. The first is that you should always believe in yourself and your abilities. The modeling industry will test your patience and resilience. Many insecure people in this industry will try to break you down and bring you to their level. Exercise patience and maintain composure. They are only a part of a bigger system. Don't let anyone, even your booker, tell you you can't. Keep your dream alive. This is your dream for life, and don't let anyone stop you.

The second thing I would like to emphasize before I end is to avoid abuse at any cost. Many people will sell their souls for fame or allow themselves to be abused for the sake of a promise that never materializes. Please, do not let that be you. You are better than that.

You can win this game by finding the right people to believe in you. Everyone can find the right people to believe in them, but it might sometimes take a little time.

Abuse comes in all forms. Do not take insults or degradation from clients or agents. A lot of models have had their self-esteems reduced to nothing that way. In the long run, you are here to win the game. Let the world be the judge, not someone who is trying to put you down so they can feel better about themself.

I hope that you will find this book useful and that it will help you to navigate the modeling terrain. If you follow the tips in this book, persevere, take action, and always be prepared, you will succeed in your modeling career.

I wish you the best, and as always, see you at the top!

Vogue Magazine Issues

Model on Photo Shoot

Models Backstage

Models on Runway

The Super Models

MODEL PLATFORMS ONLINE

www.modelmanagement.com

www.keamod.com

www.onemodelplace.com

www.modelsdirect.com

www.paidmodelingjobs.com

www.starnow.com

www.allcasting.com

www.models.com

MODEL AGENCIES
NEW YORK

APM Model Management

Website: Apmmodels.com

53 west 36th street
Newyork, NY
10018 United States

Tel: 212.966.3336
Fax: 212 925 2075

CAA

Website: caa.com

405 Lexington Ave
New York NY
10174 United States

Tel: 424 288 2000
Fax: 424 288 2900

CLICK

Website: clickmodel.com

129 West 27th Street PH
Newyork, NY
10001 United States

Tel: 212 206 1717
Fax: 212 206 6228

DNA Models Management LLC

Website: dnamodels.com

555 West 25th Street
6th Floor New York, NY
10001 United States

Tel: 212 226 0080
Fax: 212 226 2566

Elite New York City

Website: elitemodel.com

245 Fifth Avenue
24th Floor New York, NY
10016 United States

Tel: 212 529 9700
Fax: 212 475 0572

Fenton Model Management

Website: fentonmodels.com

207 East 63rd Street
#1-West New York, NY
10065 United States

Tel: 212 758 9500
Fax: 212 758 9505

Ford Models

Website: fordmodels.com

11 East 26th Street
14th Floor New York, NY
10010 United States

Tel: 212 219 6500

Fusion Models

Website: fusionmodelsnyc.com

101 North Tenth Street, Suite 301
Brooklyn, NY
11249 United States

Tel: 212 675 1300
Fax: 212 675 3289

HEROES Model Management

Website: heroesmodels.com

50 Greene Street
2nd Floor
New York, NY
10013 United States

Tel: +1 212 226 2790

IDENTITY

Website: theidentitymodels.com

110 East 25th Street
New York, NY
10010 United States

Tel: +1 646 374 4999

IMG

Website: imgmodels.com

304 Park Avenue South
12th Floor New York, NY
10010 United States

Tel: 212 253 8884
Fax: 212 253 8883

JAG Models

Website: jagmodels.com

154 West 14th St, Floor 2
New York, NY
10011 United States

Tel: 646 398 9684

Major Model Management

Website: majormodel.com

344 West 38th Street
Suite 602 New York, NY
10018 United States

Tel: 212 685 1200
Fax: 212 683 5200

Marilyn Agency

Website: marilynagency.com

32 Union Sq. East Penthouse
New York, NY
10003 United States

Tel: 212 260 6500

Muse Management

Website: musenyc.com

150 Broadway 1101
New York, NY
10038 United States

Tel: 212 625 2356

New York Model Management

Website: newyorkmodels.com

71 West 23rd Street Suite 301
New York, NY
10010 United States

Tel: 212 539 1700
Fax: 212 539 1775

Next New York

Website: nextmanagement.com

15 Watts Street 6th Floor
New York, NY
10013 United States

Tel: 212 925 5100
Fax: 212 925 5931

Official Model Management

Website: officialmodelsny.com

147 W 26th St. 3rd Floor
New York, NY
10001 United States

Tel: 646 370 1582
Fax: 646 370 1593

One Management

Website: onemanagement.com

42 Bond Street
2nd Floor New York, NY
10012 United States

Tel: 212 505 5545
Fax: 212 431 1723

Q Model Management NY

Website: qmanagementinc.com

354 Broadway
New York, NY
10013 United States

Tel: 212 807 6777
Fax: 212 807 8999

Red Model Management

Website: rednyc.com

450 W 31st 9th Floor
New York, NY
10001 United States

Tel: 212 785 1999
Fax: 212 785 1919

Soul Artist Management

Website: soulartistmanagement.com

11 West 25th Street 9th Floor
New york, NY
10010 United States

Tel: 646 827 1188

STATE Management

Website: www.statemgmt.com

525 7th Avenue Suite 904
New York, NY
10018 United States

Tel: 212 302 7792

Supreme Management

Website: suprememanagement.com

199 Lafayette Street 7th Floor
New York, NY
10012 United States

Tel: 212 334 7480
Fax: 212 334 7492

The Industry

Website: theindustrymodelmgmt.com

59 Chelsea Piers Level 3
New York, NY
10011 United States

Tel: 212 660 8800

The Lions

Website: thelionsny.com

286 5th Avenue 12th Floor
New York, NY
10001 United States

Tel: 212 226 7360
Fax: 212 226 6717

The Society Management

Website: thesocietymanagement.com

55 Hudson Yards, 3rd Floor
New York, NY
10001 United States

Tel: +1 212 377 5025
Fax: +1 212 377 5024

VNY Models

Website: vnymodels.com

928 Broadway Suite 700
New York, NY
10010 United States

Tel: 212 206 1012
Fax: 212 206 3655

Wilhelmina New York

Website: wilhelmina.com

300 Park Avenue South
New York, NY
10010 United States

Tel: 212 473 0700
Fax: 212 473 3223

Women / 360

Website: w360management.com

199 Lafayette Street #7
New York, NY
10012 United States

Tel: 646 443 9820
Fax: 646 443 9821

Women Management

Website: womenmanagement.com

55 Hudson Yards 3rd Floor
New York, NY
10001 United States

Tel: 212 334 7480
Fax: 212 334 7492

BICOASTAL MGMT

Website: bicoastalmgmt.com

1385 Broadway Ave.
Suite 1001 New york, NY
10018 United States

Tel: 212 590 0129

BMG New York

Website: bmgmodels.com

45 West 29th Street
4th Floor
New York, NY
10001 United States

Tel: 212 279 6800
Fax: 212 868 3210

Crawford Models

Website: crawfordmodels.com

34 West 37th St.
4 Floor New York, NY
10018 United States

Tel: 212 804 7292

EMG Models

Website: emgmodels.com

32 Union Sq East
10th Fl, Ste 1001
New York, NY
10003 United States

Tel: 212 505 0600

IconicFocus Models

Website: iconicfocus.com

220 Madison Ave. 6b
New York, NY
10016 United States

Tel: 516 695 6200

New Icon New York

Website: newiconny.com

220 E 23rd St. 7th Floor
New York, NY
10010 United States

Tel: +1 929 500 2400

NEW Scouting & Management

Website: newscoutingmanagement.com

Williamsburg Brooklyn, NY
11211 United States

Tel: 917 696 6103

SKorpion MGMT

Website: skorpionmgmt.com

37 West 39th St.
New York, NY
10018 United States

SOCIAL New York

Website: social-newyork.com

2 park Ave 20th Floor
New York, NY
10016 United States

Tel: 917 848 2132

The Model CoOp

Website: themodelcoop.com

246 Fifth Avenue, Suite 611
New York, NY
10001 United States

Tel: 646 633 4560

We Speak

Website: wespeakmodels.com

Fifth Ave. New York, NY
10001 United States

Tel: 917 274 7324

LONDON

3mmodels

Website: 3mmodels.com

24 Holborn Viaduct
London EC1A 2BN United Kingdom

Tel: +44 20 3239 8236

AMCK Models

Website: amckmodels.com

Penthouse
329 Latimer Road
London W10 6RA United Kingdom

Tel: +44 20 7524 7788
Fax: +44 20 7524 7789

Chapter Management

Website: chaptermgmt.co.uk

London United Kingdom

Tel: +44 0 20451 15054

D1 Model Management

Website: d1models.com

23-25 Wenlock Road
Unit 12 Union Wharf
London N1 7SB United Kingdom

Tel: +44 20 7490 8009
Fax: +44 20 7250 0889

Elite London

Website: elitemodel.co.uk

Burleigh House, 4 Floor
355 Strand London
WC2R 0HS United Kingdom

Tel: +44 0 20 7841 3288
Fax: +44 0 20 7841 3289

Established Models

Website: establishedmodels.com

16 Neals Yard First Floor
London WC2H 9DP United Kingdom

Tel: +44 203 696 9911

IMG London

Website: imgmodels.com

2 Arundel Street
London WC2R 3DA United Kingdom

Tel: +44 207 665 5500
Fax: +44 207 665 5501

Kult London

Website: kultlondon.uk

17-18 Britton Street
Level 2 London
EC1M 5NZ United Kingdom

Tel: 020 8103 4106

M + P Models

Website: mandpmodels.com

29 Poland Street
1st Floor London
W1F 8QR United Kingdom

Tel: +44 0 20 7734 1051
Fax: +44 0 20 7287 4481

Milk Management

Website: milkmanagement.co.uk

40-44 Newman Street
London W1T 1QD United Kingdom

Tel: +44 0 203 857 3690

Models 1

Website: models1.co.uk

12 Macklin Street
Covent Garden London
WC2B 4SZ United Kingdom

Tel: +44 0 20 7025 4900
Fax: + 44 0 20 7025 4901

Nevs

Website: nevsmodels.co.uk

4th Floor Broadway Studios
20 Hammersmith Broadway
London W6 7AF United Kingdom

Tel: +44 207 352 7273
Fax: +44 207 352 6068

Next London

Website: nextmanagement.com

Ground Floor Blocks B & C
Morelands Buildings 5-23 Old Street
London EC1V 9HL United Kingdom

Tel: +44 207 251 9850
Fax: +44 207 251 9851

Premier Model Management

Website: premiermodelmanagement.com

40-42 Parker Street
London WC2B 5PQ United Kingdom

Tel: +44 020 7333 0888
Fax: +44 020 7323 1221

Select Model Management London

Website: selectmodel.com

27 Mortimer Street
London W1T 3JG United Kingdom

Tel: +44 207 299 1355

Storm Management

Website: stormmanagement.com

5 Jubilee Place
London
SW3 3TD United Kingdom

Tel:+44 207 368 9967
Fax: +44 207 376 5145

Supa Model Management

Website: supamodelmanagement.com

19 Wadeson Street
London E2 9DR United Kingdom

Tel: +44 207 490 4441

TESS Management

Website: tessmanagement.com

9-10 Market Place
4th floor London
W1W 8AQ United Kingdom

Tel: +44 20 7557 7100
Fax: +44 20 7557 7101

The Squad

Website: thesquadmanagement.com

London United Kingdom

Tel: +44 203 409 9180

Viva London

Website: viva-paris.com

23 Charlotte Road
3rd Floor London
EC2A 3PB United Kingdom

Tel: +44 203 487 1240
Fax: +44 203 487 0768

Wilhelmina London

Website: wilhelmina.com

6 Perseverance Works
38 Kingsland Road
London E2 8DD United Kingdom

Tel: +44 0 20 7613 0993
Fax: +44 0 20 7613 2110

Body London

Website: bodylondon.com

1 Lyric Square
London W6 0NB United Kingdom

Tel: 0203 992 9797

FIRST Model Management

Website: firstmodelmanagement.co.uk

72 Wilton Road
London SW1V 1DE United Kingdom

Tel: 020 7436 9095

KMA

Website: katemossagency.com

25 Old Compton Street
London W1D 5JN United Kingdom

Tel: 020 3872 1200

Linden Staub

Website: lindenstaub.com

3rd Floor, 29 Charlotte Road
London EC2A 3PF United Kingdom

Tel: 0203 871 0902

Named Models

Website: namedmodels.com

5 Mandeville Courtyard
142 Battersea Park Road
London SW11 4NB United Kingdom

Tel: +44 (0) 207 652 2000

PRESENT MODEL MANAGEMENT

Website: presentmodelmanagement.com

50 Saint Aidans Road
London SE22 0RN United Kingdom

Tel: +44 07904 850 968

PRM Agency

Website: prm-agency.com

1 Gainsford Street
London SE1 2NE United Kingdom

Tel: +44 (0) 207 064 4920

The Hive Management

Website: thehivemanagement.com

Unit 17, Tileyard Studios
Tileyard Road London
N7 9AH United Kingdom

Tel: +44 (0) 203 819 7410

Titanium Management

Website: titaniummanagement.com

21 Wheler Street
London E1 6NR United Kingdom

Tel: +44 203 848 6388

Unsigned Group

Website: unsignedgrp.com

335 City Road, First Floor
London EC1V 1LJ United Kingdom

Tel: +44 (0) 203 744 7353

Wild Management

Website: WILD.MANAGEMENT

126 New Kings Road
London SW6 4LZ United Kingdom

Tel: +44 203 893 8989

MILAN

Brave Model Management

Website: bravemodels.com

Via Bordighera 2
Milan 20142 Italy

Tel: +39 02 8480 0811
Fax: +39 02 8951 1598

CREW Model Management

Website: crewmodelmanagement.com

Viale Luigi Majno, 17a
Milan 20122 Italy

Tel: +39 0 284 160 014

d'management group

Website: dmanagementgroup.com

13 via Forcella
Milan 20144 Italy

Tel: +39 02 8942 1377
Fax: +39 02 8942 1468

Elite Milan

Website: elitemodel.it

Via Tortona 35
Milan 20144 Italy

Tel: +39 02 46 75 21
Fax: +39 02 481 90 58

Fabbrica Milano Management

Website: fabbricamilano.com

Via Nirone, 2
Milan 20123 Italy

Tel: +39 02 4210 7213

Fashion Model Management

Website: fashionmodel.it

Via Guglielmo Silva, 40
Milan 20149 Italy

Tel: +39 02 48 08 61
Fax: +39 02 48 19 164

I Love Models Management

Website: ilovemodelsmanagement.com

Piazza Castello 4
Milan 20121 Italy

Tel: +39 02 00 633 530
Fax: +39 02 00 633 555

IMG Milano

Website: imgmodels.com

Via Vittoria Colonna 4
Milan 20149 Italy

Tel:+39 02 727471
Fax:+39 02 36 56 2413

Independent Model Management

Website: independentmgmt.it

Via Privata Reggio 5
Milan 20122 Italy

Tel: +39 02 8321788
Fax: +39 02 890 937 35

Monster Management

Website: monster-mgmt.com

Via Privata Paolo Giorza, 3
Milan 20144 Italy

Tel: +39 024 343 7700

Next Milan

Website: nextmanagement.com

Via Filippo Turati 40
Milan 20121 Italy
Tel; +39 02 303 5021
Fax: + 39 02 303 50281

Select Model Management Milano

Website: selectmodel.com

Via G. Washington 2
Milan 20146 Italy

Tel: +39 02 89658300
Fax: +39 02 89658398

Why Not Model Management

Website: whynotmodels.com

Via Morimondo 26
Milan 20143 Italy

Tel: +39 02 48 53 31
Fax: +39 02 481 83 44

Women Management Milan

Website: womenmanagement.it

Via Savona 58
Milan 20143 Italy

Tel: +39 0 2477 195 57
Fax: +39 0 2422 906 72

Angels & Demons Models

Website: rsbmilanomanagement.com

Via Dezza, 47
Milan 20144 Italy

Tel: +39 023 669 6381

BOOM Models Agency

Website: boomtheagency.it

Corso Lodi 12
Milan 20135 Italy

Tel: +39 023 672 3773
Fax: +39 023 672 3789

E2 Model Management

Website: e2modelmanagement.com

Via Rodolfo Farneti 1
Milan 20129 Italy

Tel: +39 392 390 0948

Major Models Milan

Website: majormilano.it

Via Seprio 2
2nd Floor Milan 20149 Italy

Tel: +39 024 801 2840
Fax: +39 024 819 4081

NOLOGO MGMT

Website: nologomgmt.com

Via Delle Stelline - 1
Milan 20146 Italy

Tel: +39 02 833 0101
Fax: +39 028 330 1030

PWR MODELS

Website: pwrmodels.com

Corso di Porta Romana
129 Milan 20122 Italy

Tel: + 39 029 127 0200

Special Management

Website: specialmanagement.it

Via Revere 11
Milan 20123 Italy

Tel: +39 023 658 0281

The Lab Models

Website: thelabmodels.com

Via Luigi Cagnola
8 Milan 20154 Italy

Tel: +39 023 670 4840

URBN Models

Website: urbnmodels.com

Via Tortona 16
Milan 20144 Italy

Tel: + 39 028 324 1415
Fax: + 39 028 324 9570

Wave Management/The Wall

Website: wavemanagement.it

Via Alberto Mario 26
Milan 20149 Italy
Tel; +39 022 111 8545

Women Direct

Website: womendirect.it

Via Savona 58
Milan 20144 Italy

Tel: +39 024 771 9557

Wonderwall Management

Website: ww-mgmt.com

Via Privata Paolo Giorza 3
Milan 20144 Italy

Tel: +39 024 343 7220

PARIS

16 & 16 MEN

Website: 16men.com

5 Rue Abel
Paris 75012 France

Tel: 01 40 26 12 76

Bananas Models

Website: bananasmodels.com

9 Rue Duphot
Paris 75001 France

Tel: +33 (0) 1 40 20 02 03
Fax: +33 (0) 1 40 20 41 20

Elite Paris

Website: elitemodel.fr

19 Avenue George V
Paris 75008 France

Tel: +33 1 40 44 32 22
Fax: +33 1 44 44 32 80

Ford Models Paris

Website: fordmodels.com

278 Boulevard Saint Germain
Paris 75007 France

Tel: +33 1 44 18 08 08

IMG Paris

Website: imgmodels.com

20 Rue de La Baume
Paris 75008 France

Tel: +33 1 55 35 12 00
Fax: +33 1 55 35 12 01

Karin Models

Website: karinmodelsparis.com

9 Avenue Hoche
Paris 75008 France

Tel: +33 1 45 63 08 23
Fax: +33 1 45 63 58 18

Marilyn Agency

Website: marilynagency.com

11 Rue Portefoin
Paris 75003 France

Tel: +33 1 53 29 53 53
Fax: +33 1 53 29 53 00

Metropolitan/M Management/Makers

Website: metropolitanmodels.com

37 Bis Avenue d'Iena
Paris 75116 France

Tel: +33 1 42 66 52 85
Fax: +33 1 42 66 48 75

New Madison

Website: newmadison.fr

10 Rue Aux Ours
Paris 75003 France

Tel: +33 0 1 44 29 29 16
Fax: +33 0 1 44 29 01 64

Next Paris

Website: nextmanagement.com

9 Boulevard de La Madeleine
Paris 75001 France

Tel: +33 1 5345 1300
Fax: +33 1 5345 1301

Oui Management

Website: ouimanagement.com

20 Passage Dauphine
Paris 75006 France

Tel: +33 1 4326 3232
Fax: +33 1 7270 3939

Premium Models

Website: premium-models.com

3 Rue de Choiseul
Paris 75002 France

Tel: +33 1 53 05 25 25
Fax: +33 1 53 05 25 26

Rock Men

Website: rockmen.fr

6 Rue Saint Claude
Paris 75003 France

Tel: +33 1 72 74 15 30

SAFE Mgmt

Website: safemgmt.com

Paris 75004 France

Tel: +3 364 843 9655

Select Model Management Paris

Website: selectmodel.com

14 Rue Favart
Paris 75002 France

Tel: +33 0 1 40 20 15 15
Fax: +33 0 1 40 20 15 10

Success Models

Website: successmodels.com

11-13 Rue des Arquesbusiers
Paris 75003 France

Tel: +33 0 1 42 78 89 89
Fax: +33 0 1 42 78 80 02

Supreme Management

Website: suprememanagement.fr

3 Rue Meyerbeer
Paris 75009 France

Tel: +33 1 77 45 55 10
Fax: +331 77 45 55 11

The Claw

Website: theclawmodels.com

38 Rue du Louvre
Paris 75001 France

Tel: +33 1 45 35 32 09

Viva Paris

Website: viva-paris.com

Beau Passage
53-57 rue de Grenelle
Paris 75007 France

Tel: +33 1 44 55 12 60
Fax: +33 1 44 55 12 62

City Models

Website: city-models.com

32 Rue de Penthièvre
Paris 75008 France

Tel: +33 1 53 93 33 33
Fax: +33 1 53 93 33 34

COVER

Website: cover.paris

6 Rue Saint Claude
Paris 75003 France

Tel: 33 1 72 74 15 20

Maxence Orard

Website: maxenceorard.com

Paris 75018 France

Silent

Website: silentmodels.com

54 Rue Ponthieu
Paris 75008 France

Tel: +33 1 780 954 40
Fax: +33 1 780 954 41

Silver

Website: agencesilver.com

6 Rue Saint Claude
Paris 75003 France

Tel: +33140204365

The Face

Website: thefaceparis.com

23 Rue d'Antin
Paris 75002 France

Tel: 01 76 21 76 30

Titanium Management

Website: titaniummanagement.com

51 Rue Greneta
Paris 75002 France

Tel: 33 1 87 89 85 41

Women 360 Paris

Website: w360management.fr

3 Rue Meyerbeer
4th & 5th Floor
Paris 75009 France

Tel: +33 1 77 45 55 19

MADRID

Wild Mgmt

Website: wildmgmt.es

Plaza Alonso Martinez 7
1º Derecha
Madrid 28004 Spain

Tel: +34682392775

TOKYO

Bon Image Corp.

Website: image-tokyo.co.jp

1-15-14-8 Minamiaoyama Minato-ku
Tokyo 107-0062 Japan

Tel: +81 3 3403 4110
Fax: +81 3 3403 4662

Bravo Models

Website: bravomodels.net

Hillside Terrace H301
18-17 Sarugakucho, Shibuya-ku
Tokyo 150-0033 Japan

Tel: +81-3-3463-9090
Fax: +81-3-3463-9091

Donna Models

Website: donnamodels.jp

Jinnan Plaza #603
1.15.3 Jinnan Shibuya-ku
Tokyo 150-0041 Japan

Tel: +81 03 3770 8255
Fax: +81 03 3770 8266

Unknown Model Management

Website: unknownmodels.co.jp

NC Bldg 6F-B 1-9-4 Jinnan Shibuya-ku
Tokyo 150-0041 Japan

Tel: +81-3-6427-0314

CDU Models

Website: cdumodels.com

Al Bergo Nogizaka 508, 9-6-28 Akasaka
Minato-ku Tokyo 107-0052 Japan

Tel: +81 3 3402 8445

Exiles Models

Website: exileshype.com

6F Maruei BLDG
1-9-7 Jinnan, Shibuya
Tokyo 150 0041 Japan

Satoru Japan Inc.

Website: satorujapan.co.jp

7F 6-12-1 MinamiAoyama Minato-ku
Tokyo 107-0062 Japan

Tel: +81-3-3498-9000

TOKYO REBELS, Inc.

Website: tokyo-rebels.com

2-10-1F Kamiyamacho
Shibuya-ku
Tokyo 150-0047 Japan

Tel: +813-5738-7858
Fax: +81 3 3465 4871

WEST Management Tokyo

Website: west-management.jp

Uehara 1-7-19, Shibuya-ku
Tokyo 151-0064 Japan

Tel: 81 3 6427 8626

Wizard Models

Website: wizardmodels.com

5B Futaba Bld, 1-16-6,
Dogenzaka, Shibuya-ku
Tokyo 150-0043 Japan

Tel: +81-3-5728-8366

CAPE TOWN

20 Model Management

Website: 20management.co.za

B202 Buchanan Square
160 Sir Lowry Road
Cape Town 7925 South Africa

Tel: +27 21 462 0120

Boss Models Cape Town

Website: bossmodels.co.za

220 Buitengracht Street,
Cape Town 8001 South Africa

Tel: 27 21 424 0224

Fax: 27 21 423 6967

LOS ANGELES

IMG Los Angeles

Website: imgmodels.com

700 N. San Vicente Blvd.
Suite G600, 6th Floor
Los Angeles 90069 United States

Tel: 1 310 550 3405

LA Model Management

Website: lamodels.com

7700 Sunset Blvd.
Los Angeles, CA
90046 United States

Tel: 323 436 7700
Fax: 323 436 7755

Next LA

Website: nextmanagement.com

8447 Wilshire Boulevard
PH Suite
Los Angeles, CA
90211 United States

Tel: 323 782 0010
Fax: 323 782 0035

No Ties Management

Website: notiesmanagement.com

434 W Cedar St.
San Diego, CA
92101 United States

Tel: 619.819.9168
Fax: 619 819 6119

Photogenics LA

Website: photogenicsmedia.com

3103 A S La Cienega Blvd
Los Angeles, CA
90016 United States

STATE Management

Website: statemgmt.com

8075 West 3rd Street
Suite #307
Los Angeles, CA
90048 United States

Tel: (323) 908 0051

Storm Management

Website: stormmanagement-la.com

8797 Beverly Blvd
Los Angeles, CA
90048 United States

Tel: 424 288 4861

Two Management

Website: twomanagement.com

8000 Sunset Blvd.
Suite A201
Los Angeles, CA
90046 United States

VISION Los Angeles

Website: visionlosangeles.com

8631 Washington Blvd.
Los Angeles, CA
90232 United States

Tel: 310 733 4440
Fax: 310 733 4441

Elite LA

Website: elitemodel.com

518 N La Cienega Blvd.
West Hollywood, CA
90048 United States

Tel: 310 274 9395
Fax: 310 278 7520

Ford Models LA

Website: fordmodels.com

9200 Sunset Boulevard
Suite 817
West Hollywood, CA
90069 United States

Tel: 310 276 8100
Fax: 310 276 9299

Freedom Models

Website: freedommodels.com

820 N. Fairfax Avenue
Los Angeles, CA
90046 United States

Tel: 213 261 3810

Nomad Management

Website: nomadmgmt.com

8335 Sunset Blvd.
Suite 325
West Hollywood, CA
90069 United States

Tel: 310 730 5456

Nous Model Management

Website: nousmodels.com

6300 Wilshire Blvd, #970
Los Angeles, CA
90048 United States

Tel: 310 385 6900
Fax: 310 385 6910

Scout Model Agency

Website: scouttm.com

6363 Wilshire Boulevard
#400 Los Angeles, CA
90048 United States

Tel: 310 274 2779

Select Model Management Los Angeles

Website: selectmodel.com

7250 Melrose Ave.
#4 Los Angeles, CA
90046 United States

SOCIAL New York

Website: social-newyork.com

1601 Vine Street
Los Angeles, CA
90028 United States

Tel: 917 848 2132

The Industry LA

Website: theindustrymodelmgmt.com

469 South Robertson Blvd.
Beverly Hills, CA
90211 United States

Tel: 310 691 7900

HONG KONG

Tigers by Matt

Website: tigersbymatt.com

Amtel Building
14/F des Voeux Road Central HK
Hong Kong
Hong Kong

Tel: +39 329 709 5213

ATHENS

Ace Models

Website: www.acemodels.gr

3 Makrigianni Str.
Athens 11742 Greece

Tel: +30 210 922 6200
Fax: +30 210 924 4636

Agencia Models

Website: www.agencia.gr

Kleomenous 39A
Athens 10676 Greece

Tel: +210 689 2761

D Model Agency

Website: www.dmodelagency.com

Evripidou 30
Athens 10551 Greece

Tel: 003 021 0922 8707